Here Comes Winter

QUILTED PROJECTS TO WARM YOUR HOME

Jeanne Large and Shelley Wicks

Martingale®
Create with Confidence

Here Comes Winter:
Quilted Projects to Warm Your Home
© 2014 by Jeanne Large and Shelley Wicks

Martingale®
19021 120th Ave. NE, Ste. 102
Bothell, WA 98011-9511 USA
ShopMartingale.com

Printed in China
19 18 17 16 15 14   8 7 6 5 4 3 2 1

**Library of Congress Cataloging-in-Publication Data
is available upon request.**

ISBN: 978-1-60468-371-4

5571 9354   *08/14*

MISSION STATEMENT

Dedicated to providing quality products and service
to inspire creativity.

CREDITS

PRESIDENT AND CEO: Tom Wierzbicki
EDITOR IN CHIEF: Mary V. Green
DESIGN DIRECTOR: Paula Schlosser
MANAGING EDITOR: Karen Costello Soltys
ACQUISITIONS EDITOR: Karen M. Burns
TECHNICAL EDITOR: Ellen Pahl
COPY EDITOR: Tiffany Mottet
PRODUCTION MANAGER: Regina Girard
COVER AND INTERIOR DESIGNER: Adrienne Smitke
PHOTOGRAPHER: Brent Kane
ILLUSTRATOR: Rose Wright

Contents

Bonus Pattern Online!

Visit ShopMartingale.com/Extras to download
"Snowstorm Stitchery" for free.

Introduction

Ahhhh, the winter season again. Where we live, winter can be six or seven months long, so it's truly a season to embrace! Most of our quilts and projects are a celebration of winter as a season rather than Christmas as a holiday. We make our homes cozy and inviting during this time of year with winter quilts, pillows, and runners, often incorporating snowmen. Everyone loves snowmen, no matter where they live. A quilt with a snowman can add a touch of whimsy to your decorating and, whether big or small, it will be a great conversation piece.

The first snowfall is our cue to pull out our winter quilts with snowmen and snowflakes. It's great to have a few lap quilts handy to snuggle under as the temperature drops. Then as the holiday season creeps closer, we can add the festive quilts and table toppers. These items really make a home look ready for Christmas.

We love the scents of the holiday season as well. You can fill your home with a wonderful fragrance by adding cinnamon sticks, cloves, and orange slices to a slow cooker full of water. Turn the heat to low, and when the mixture is warm, leave the lid off and enjoy the aroma. Keep an eye on the water level, refilling when it gets low. You don't want the water to completely evaporate.

Winter is a wonderful time to gather your friends for a fabric or block exchange. A day of sewing with friends can revive your interest in a project and refill your creative energy tank to get you off and running on something new. You could choose a block for everyone to sew and make as many as possible in a day of sewing, eating, and visiting. At the end of the day, share the blocks so everyone has a "piece" of the day to take home. A sewing day with friends is a fabulous way to share ideas, tips, and information about quilting, holiday decorating, and life in general.

We have learned that love, friendship, and a good quilt will help make winter a season to celebrate.

Basic Quiltmaking Techniques

A good basic skill is like riding a bike—you usually don't forget how, but it's always good to have a grasp on the fundamentals, just in case. So whether you are new to quilting, or have the skills and just want to brush up, this section is for you.

FABRIC SELECTION AND PREPARATION

We can't stress enough the importance of embarking on a project with the best-quality fabrics you can find—quilt-shop quality. Making a quilt takes the same amount of time, whatever the fabric quality. The difference is, the one made with top-quality fabric will last longer, look better, and generally stand the test of time. Isn't that something you would want—especially if you plan to give your quilt as a gift? We think so.

With regard to prewashing your fabric, never has there been such a controversial or confusing topic. Many quilters don't know which camp they should be in. We can tell you that we are in the "don't prewash camp." That's right—we don't prewash our fabrics. And you know what? The quilting police have not come to take us away yet!

We all have a lot of laundry to do already, so why add to the load? (Pardon the pun!) The fabric manufactured today doesn't have the shrink rate it did even 20 years ago. The dye is much more stable, so unless you are using a hand-dyed fabric, dye bleed shouldn't be an issue. (With that said, let a quilt sit somewhere soaking wet and you will almost always have trouble!) The sizing that is in the fabric when you purchase it also makes for a crisp feel and easier handling.

When shopping for fabric, we now have access to all varieties of precuts, 5" squares, 10" squares, 2½"-wide strips, and much more. These items are not meant to be prewashed, and to do so is asking for trouble. These items will simply fray too much to be manageable. Besides, who wants to iron ragged squares and shaggy strips into submission?

Another thing you should avoid is prewashing a quilt top before quilting. That's a recipe for disaster. You'll end up with open seams, threads hanging everywhere, and depending on the type of fabric, maybe some very frayed edges. And you certainly will have to iron the quilt top before you could even think about basting and quilting it.

We don't prewash our quilt batting or our fabric for backing either. If you really feel the need to wash the quilt, do it after the quilt is layered, quilted, and bound. That way, the quilt top, batting, and backing will shrink (a minimal amount) together to give you that overall soft scrunchiness that says, "Use me!"

ROTARY-CUTTING TOOLS

All the projects in this book require the basic tools of quiltmaking: a rotary cutter, mat, and ruler. You have many brands and sizes to choose from, so you must decide what will suit your needs and your budget. While there are very inexpensive tools out there, generally, you will get what you pay for. And while a great deal is fabulous, if you have to repurchase that same product every year, it's not really such a deal after all. The best place to buy your tools, in our opinion, is at your local quilt shop. The knowledgeable staff will be able to direct you to what will best meet your needs.

Some quilters like to purchase every tool and ruler that hits the market, but for starting out, we suggest one ruler, 6" x 24". This will accommodate most cutting, and makes it easy to cut your fabric as it comes folded from the bolt. As for a rotary cutter, it's really a matter of preference, but again, remember the rule, you get what you pay for. We prefer the 45 mm size. It's a standard size and by far the most practical for starting out.

Your cutting mat need not be large, but having said that, we encourage you to purchase the largest size you can afford and have space for. A large mat will allow you to cut several strips without having to move the fabric or fold it over more than once.

ROTARY-CUTTING BASICS

Accurate cutting is the first step in precise piecing, and the most important step is to begin with a straight edge. This may be referred to as "squaring up your fabric."

1. Fold the fabric in half, lining up the selvages. Lay the fabric on the cutting mat with the selvages closest to you and align them with a horizontal line on your mat. Line the left edge of the fabric along the left edge of the mat, being sure both raw edges are just over the edge of the mat, and the rest of the fabric is to your right. This is where the 6" x 24" ruler is the most convenient size to have. If you are left-handed, cut with the fabric to your left, and cut on the left side of the ruler.

2. Lay the ruler along a vertical line on your mat so that all the raw edges of the fabric are covered by the ruler. Place your hand firmly on the ruler, letting your pinkie finger rest against the outer edge to prevent slipping. Use the rotary cutter to cut along the right side of the ruler, keeping even pressure on your rotary cutter through the full length of the cut. Discard the small strip of fabric that you just cut off. Your fabric is now straightened and ready to cut.

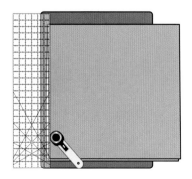

3. Use the straightened edge as a starting point to measure and cut strips as required by the pattern instructions. For added accuracy, we like to use the lines on the mat as well as the lines on the ruler. For example, to cut a strip 2½" wide, place the 2½" vertical line of the ruler along the straightened edge of the fabric, also making sure the ruler is lined up with the vertical lines on the mat.

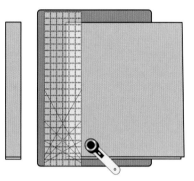

4. To crosscut strips into squares or rectangles, open up the folded strip and place it along a horizontal line on the mat. Trim off the selvage. Measure and cut from the trimmed edge, lining up the desired line of the ruler with the trimmed edge and with the lines on your mat.

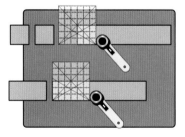

ACCURATE PIECING

An accurate ¼" seam allowance is a key factor in quilting. Accurate piecing will ensure that your blocks fit together and you will be happy with the finished product. Even a very small amount of error will multiply until your rows won't fit together like they should. Many sewing machines come with a ¼" presser foot. If your machine doesn't have one, it's easy to make a guide on your machine with quilter's ¼" masking tape.

Place an acrylic ruler under your presser foot. Line up the edge of the ruler with the edge of the presser foot. Be sure the ruler is straight. Gently lower the needle. Move the ruler until the needle lines up with the ¼" mark on the ruler. Lay a piece of masking tape along the edge of the ruler to mark the alignment, being careful not to cover the feed dogs with tape. Use this taped line as a guide when feeding fabric through the machine and you should have an accurate ¼" seam allowance.

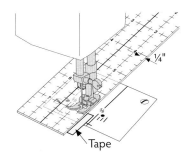

STRIP PIECING

Strip-piecing techniques can speed up the piecing process and are very useful when making checkerboard blocks or anything with numerous repetitive pieces.

To make a strip set, sew strips together in the required fabric combinations. Press the seam allowances toward the darker fabric, or as indicated in the project instructions. Place the strip set on your cutting mat, straighten one end, and cut into the required-size segments.

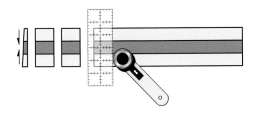

CHAIN PIECING

When piecing multiple units that are the same, chain piece them by feeding the units through your machine continuously, without stopping to cut the thread between each one. When the units are all sewn, remove the chain and snip the threads between each unit. Press according to your pattern instructions. This is a great timesaving technique, and something you will become more proficient at as you do more quilting.

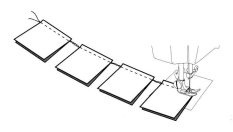

PRESSING

Careful pressing is just as important as accurate piecing to ensure that your quilt top finishes at the correct size and comes together smoothly. Good pressing techniques will help your blocks lie flat and fit together well.

Steam or dry iron? There are various opinions on this. We prefer an iron that steams well. However, be careful not to stretch your blocks when using the steam setting. If your block is a bit misshapen, a good spray starch and some steam can work wonders.

1. Lay the pieced unit on the ironing board with the fabric that you want to press the seam allowances toward positioned on top. Unless your pattern tells you otherwise, press seam allowances toward the darker fabric. Place the iron onto the sewn seam very briefly to set the seam.

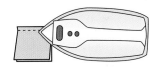

2. Lift the iron and open the unit by lifting the top piece of fabric and folding it over the seam allowances. Press the seam flat from the right side. The seam allowances will lie flat under the fabric that was originally positioned on top.

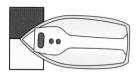

When sewing blocks together into rows, press the seam allowances in opposite directions from one row to the next. This makes it easier to nest the seam allowances of the blocks together when joining the rows. Your seams will lie flat and give you a smooth finish on the front of your quilt.

FUSIBLE APPLIQUÉ

Appliqué can elevate a simple quilt to a superb quilt in no time at all. Appliqué doesn't have to be small and intricate to add impact. We prefer our appliqué to be big and bold and to make a statement! Plus, we use fusible appliqué to make the process quick and easy.

With so many fusible products on the market, it's important to find the one that will work best for your project. We highly recommend a lightweight product, no matter what brand you decide is right for you. A heavier weight tends to gum up your sewing-machine needle, is harder to sew through, and adds a stiff feeling to your quilts. Be sure to read the instructions that come with the product you are using. Each one has different guidelines for heat settings and fusing times.

When using fusible web, the patterns must be the reverse of the finished shape. The patterns in this book have all been reversed for you.

1. Trace the appliqué patterns onto the paper side of the fusible product using a pencil and leaving about 1" between shapes.

2. Cut the appliqué shapes out of the fusible web, approximately ¼" outside of the pencil lines. If the shape is large, cut out the fusible web from the center of each piece, leaving ¼" to ½" inside the pencil line. This helps to keep the appliqué pieces soft in the finished quilt.

3. Following the manufacturer's instructions, fuse each shape, paper side up, onto the wrong side of the desired fabric. Press carefully using an up-and-down motion. You don't want your shapes to slide around.

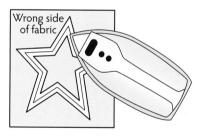

4. Allow the fabrics to cool and then cut out each appliqué piece directly on the drawn line. Remove the paper backing from each piece.

5. Use your ironing board as a work surface to arrange the shapes onto the background fabric or blocks. Refer to the pattern for proper placement so you can be sure all shapes are tucked under or overlapped where they should be. Fuse the appliqués in place.

6. Sew the raw edges of all the appliqué shapes to the background fabric either by hand or machine. We like to use a blanket stitch. Using a thread color that matches the appliqué pieces will make your stitching almost invisible. Using a dark-charcoal or black thread gives a more primitive look.

SPECIAL TECHNIQUES

Taking the time to add a little extra zing to your project is often what makes it shine. Adding something special doesn't have to be difficult. Often the simplest additions add the most pizzazz to a project. In this section, you'll find the fun techniques we've used in the projects throughout the book.

Using Rickrack

Rickrack makes a wonderful vine, flower stem, or accent on a quilt. It comes in a variety of widths and a wide range of colors, so you have plenty of options.

You also have several options when sewing rickrack to your project. If you are using a narrow product, just pin the rickrack in place and sew through the center of the strip by machine. It's a good idea to use a walking foot for doing this to avoid stretching the rickrack. If you're using wide rickrack, sew the edges down on both sides so they won't roll up or distort in any way when your quilt is washed. Sew the edges using a machine blanket stitch or a straight stitch, or use our favorite method—drop your feed dogs and free-motion stitch the edges with matching thread.

Hand Embroidery

A fine pearl cotton or two strands of embroidery floss work well for the simple hand stitches we use on our quilts. Be sure to use an embroidery needle with a large eye. The stitching is always done before the quilt top is layered, basted, and quilted, so the back of your work is hidden. If you're worried about the knots and threads from the back of your work showing through to the front when finished, place a piece of muslin behind your work and stitch through both layers. This will not only hide any loose threads on the back of your work, but also add more stability to the area being stitched.

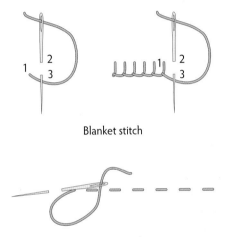

Blanket stitch

Running stitch

Machine Embroidery

Sometimes you just don't want to take the time for hand stitching, or maybe you simply don't enjoy hand embroidery. In these cases, we've come up with an easy machine-stitching method that works quite nicely.

Use a thread color that reflects the item you are stitching. For example, in this book, we used a dark-brown thread for reindeer antlers and eyes. Drop the feed dogs on your machine and free-motion stitch the antlers, going over the shape of the antlers two or three times. For the eyes, simply go around in circles until you've achieved the size of eye you want. Practice this technique on scraps before moving on to your project.

Framing a Project

If you're planning to frame a finished project, it's a good idea to define your parameters before you start to ensure your work will fit into the frame you have chosen. For instance, if you're appliquéing onto a background fabric, use a piece of chalk to draw lines that indicate the inside edge of the frame.

You can do this by tracing around the glass from the frame or measuring and drawing with a ruler. This will make the placement of the appliqué shapes easier and will also help when it's time to put your work into the frame. Trim the background fabric to be 2" larger than your drawn line on all sides. When your piece is complete, follow the steps below to frame it.

1. Remove the backing from the frame. Cut a piece of thin cardboard or mat board the same size as the glass in the frame.

2. Lay your completed work facedown, and center the cardboard on the back of it. Fold the top and bottom edges of your project onto the cardboard and use masking tape to hold them in place. Lift up and check to see how it looks from the front to be sure your project is centered and not distorted.

3. Fold the sides to the back and tape to the cardboard. Check the front again, and be sure your project is stretched firmly around the cardboard.

4. Clean the right side of your project with a lint roller and clean the inside of the glass with a glass cleaner. Let the glass air dry to be sure no moisture becomes trapped inside your framed piece.

5. Place the project onto the glass through the back of the frame.

6. Replace the backing onto the frame and fasten in place. Voilà! A unique piece of art by you!

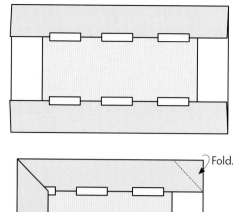

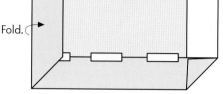

Framing Tips

* Consider the style of your specific project when choosing a frame.
* Using the mat that comes in the frame is only an option. The frame size without the mat may work better for you.
* Framing without a mat will give the piece a more primitive look.
* Use the frame without the glass if you plan to embellish your work with beads and buttons.
* You can always have your work custom framed. A frame shop has the knowledge and equipment to make your work look professional.

ADDING BORDERS

When your quilt top is complete and it's time to add the borders, measure your quilt top to ensure that the size of borders the pattern tells you to cut is in fact what your quilt top measures. Sometimes the difference in seam allowances can add a bit of discrepancy in the finished size of the quilt top.

Careful measuring will ensure that your quilt top will lie flat. Double-checking your measurements and adjusting the border lengths accordingly can avoid borders that are too tight or fall in waves. Be sure your quilt top is pressed well before measuring.

1. Lay the quilt top out flat and measure through the vertical center and both sides, about 6" in from the edges. If the measurements differ from each other, take the average of the three measurements and cut the two vertical borders to that length.

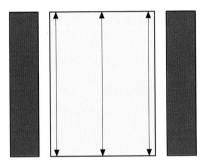

2. Fold these border strips in half crosswise to find the center. Do the same with the quilt top. Pin the center of the border to the center of the side of the quilt top. Align the ends of the quilt top and the ends of the border, and pin in place. Add more pins between these pinpoints, easing in any fullness or gently stretching as required.

3. Sew the border strips to the sides of the quilt top. Press.

4. Repeat the process for the top and bottom borders, measuring through the horizontal center and sides.

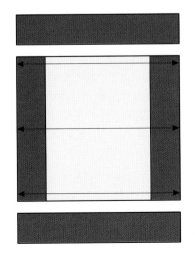

BINDING

All of our projects include a double-fold binding made from 2½"-wide strips. The patterns in this book allow for enough binding to go around the perimeter of the quilt, plus 12" extra for joining the strips and mitering corners.

1. Cut the binding fabric across the width, unless otherwise specified, into the required number of 2½"-wide strips.

2. With right sides together, join the binding strips at right angles as shown to make one long strip. Trim seam allowances to ¼" and press them open to reduce bulk.

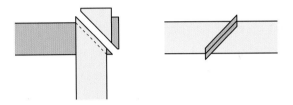

3. Fold the binding in half widthwise with wrong sides together and press.

4. Place the end of the binding midway down one edge of the quilt. Align the binding raw edges with the edge of the quilt top and start sewing approximately 10" from the start of the binding strip. Sew through all the layers using a ¼" seam allowance, stopping ¼" from the first corner. Backstitch, clip the threads, and remove the quilt from the machine.

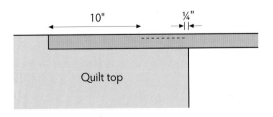

5. Turn the quilt so you're ready to sew the next side. Fold the binding straight up at a 90° angle away from the quilt, and then back down on itself so the binding raw edge is even with the quilt edge again. Stitch from the fold, backstitching at the edge of the quilt. This fold will create a mitered corner when you turn the binding to the back of the quilt and blindstitch it in place. Continue sewing the binding to the edges of the quilt, repeating the mitering process at the remaining corners.

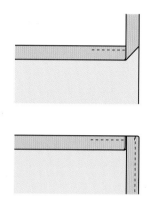

6. Stop sewing and backstitch when you are approximately 10" to 12" from where you started. Take the quilt out of the machine. Measure out a 2½" overlap of binding fabric. Trim off excess fabric. (The overlap should measure the same width as the cut binding.)

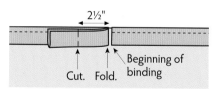

7. Open up the binding strips. Pin the right end of the binding strip to the left end, right sides together and perpendicular to each other. Sew on the diagonal and trim the excess fabric. Press the seam allowances open. Fold the binding in half widthwise again and align the binding strip to the edge of the quilt. Finish sewing the binding in place.

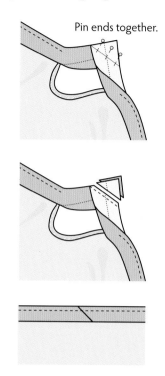

8. Bring the folded edge of the binding over to the back of the quilt, covering the raw edges of the quilt and the line of stitching. Use a thread that matches the binding and blindstitch in place, mitering each corner as you come to it.

BIAS BINDING

A bias binding is easy to curve and manipulate because the strips are cut at a 45° angle to the straight of grain. Use it for binding curves or when you want a plaid or stripe fabric to be on the bias.

1. Lay your fabric along the cutting mat and cut the fabric diagonally, using the 45° line on your ruler or cutting mat as a guideline. Using the diagonal line you have just cut as your guide, continue to cut 2½"-wide diagonal strips of fabric.

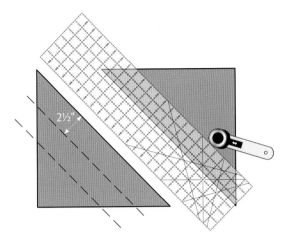

2. Sew the strips together to achieve the length required. With right sides together, join the strips at right angles as shown. Pressing the seam allowances open will reduce the amount of bulk at those spots.

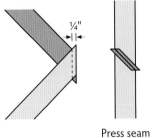

Press seam
allowances open.

3. Lay the strip right side down on your ironing board. Fold it in half widthwise and press with wrong sides together.

4. Sew the binding to the raw edge of the quilt in the same manner as for straight-grain binding. Gently curve the binding—without stretching it—around the curved portion of the project.

"Crosswalk," designed and pieced by Jeanne Large and Shelley Wicks, machine quilted by Wendy Findlay.

Crosswalk

*W*elcome *winter with this quick and easy quilt. This is one of those projects that you can make many times over, in various colorways, so choose red or any favorite color. Whether you make this for a special someone or just to use your stash, the end result is an appealing quilt that looks far more complicated than it really is.*

FINISHED QUILT: 56½" x 70½" ◆ FINISHED BLOCK: 14" x 14"

MATERIALS

Yardage is based on 42"-wide fabric. Fat quarters measure approximately 18" x 21".

14 fat quarters of assorted red prints for blocks

2 yards of beige print for block background

⅝ yard of red print for binding

3⅔ yards of fabric for backing

65" x 79" piece of batting

CUTTING

Cut all strips across the width of the fabric.

From *each* of the red fat quarters, cut:

5 strips, 3" x 21"; crosscut the strips into
  29 squares, 3" x 3" (406 total, 6 are extra)

From the beige print, cut:

5 strips, 8⅜" x 42"; crosscut the strips into
  20 squares, 8⅜" x 8⅜". Cut each square into
  quarters diagonally to yield 80 triangles.

5 strips, 4½" x 42"; crosscut the strips into
  40 squares, 4½" x 4½". Cut each square in half
  diagonally to yield 80 triangles.

From the red print, cut:

7 strips, 2½" x 42"

PIECING THE BLOCKS

1. Sew four different red 3" squares together in pairs. Press the seam allowances in opposite directions for each. Sew the pairs together to make a four-patch unit. Make 100 four-patch units.

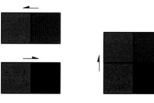

Make 100.

2. Sew three of the four-patch units together. Press the seam allowances toward the center unit. Make 20 of these units.

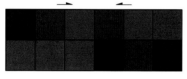

Make 20.

3. Sew beige 8⅜" triangles to opposite sides of the remaining four-patch units. The bottom of the triangle will line up with the bottom of the four-patch unit and the point of the triangle will be slightly longer than the four-patch unit. Press the seam allowances toward the triangles. Make 40 of these units.

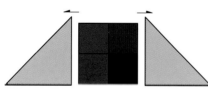

Make 40.

4. Lay out two units from step 3 together with a unit from step 2 as shown and sew the units together. Press the seam allowances toward the step 3 units.

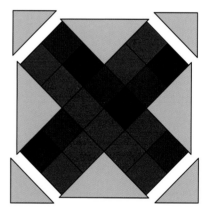

5. Sew a beige 4½" triangle to each corner of the block. Press the seam allowances toward the corner triangles. Make 20 blocks.

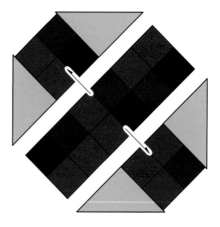

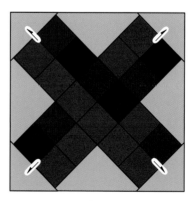

Make 20.

6. Trim each block to measure 14½" x 14½". Be sure to leave ¼" seam allowance beyond the points so they will match up when you sew the blocks together.

ASSEMBLING THE QUILT TOP

1. Arrange the blocks into five rows of four blocks each as shown. Sew the blocks together, aligning the seams as you sew. Press the seam allowances open to eliminate bulk.

2. Sew the rows together. Press the seam allowances open.

Quilt assembly

FINISHING THE QUILT

1. Layer the backing, batting, and quilt top; baste.

2. Quilt as desired. Our quilt is machine quilted with an allover design.

3. Bind the quilt using the red 2½"-wide strips. Refer to "Binding" on page 11 as needed.

"Hang to Dry," designed and made by Shelley Wicks and Jeanne Large, machine quilted by Wendy Findlay.

Hang to Dry

*C*uddle up under this fun quilt all winter long. The snowmen holding up the rickrack clothesline are peeking over the Rail Fence blocks while waiting for their mittens to dry. They're sure to make you feel warm on a chilly evening.

FINISHED QUILT: 54½" x 72½" ◆ FINISHED BLOCK: 8" x 8"

MATERIALS

Yardage is based on 42"-wide fabric. Fat quarters measure approximately 18" x 21".

1½ yards of dark-brown print for sashing, border, and binding

⅜ yard *each* of 2 brown, 2 red, 2 green, and 2 blue prints for Rail Fence blocks

6 fat quarters of assorted beige prints for appliqué background

9" x 14" piece of black flannel for hats

7" x 17" piece of gold flannel for stars

7" x 14" piece of white flannel for snowmen

7" x 12" piece of red flannel #1 for hatbands and scarves

7" x 12" piece of green flannel for holly leaves

5" x 16" piece of brown flannel for arms

6" x 10" piece *each* of 2 different red flannels (#2 and #3) for mittens

6" x 10" piece *each* of 2 different blue flannels for mittens

4" x 6" piece of orange flannel for noses

3½ yards of fabric for backing

63" x 81" piece of batting

3⅓ yards of ½"-wide green rickrack

1¾ yards of 18"-wide lightweight fusible web

Matching thread for appliqué

6 red buttons, ½" diameter, for holly berries

4 black buttons, ¼" diameter, for snowman eyes

4 red buttons, ⅝" diameter, for mittens

4 blue buttons, ⅝" diameter, for mittens

CUTTING

Cut all strips across the width of the fabric.

From *each* of the brown, red, green, and blue prints, cut:
1 strip, 3" x 42" (8 total)
1 strip, 2" x 42" (8 total)
2 strips, 2½" x 42" (16 total)

From *each* of the beige fat quarters, cut:
2 strips, 6½" x 21"; crosscut the strips into 6 squares, 6½" x 6½" (36 total, 4 are extra)

From the dark-brown print, cut:
5 strips, 1" x 42"
7 strips, 3½" x 42"
7 strips, 2½" x 42"

2. Arrange the blocks into five rows with six blocks in each row, rotating the blocks to form the rail fence design as shown. Sew the blocks into rows, pressing the seam allowances to one side. Sew two rows together. Press the seam allowances in one direction. Make two sections of two rows each. The remaining row will be the center row in the quilt.

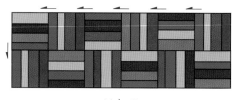

Make 1.

Make 2.

3. Lay out eight beige 6½" squares. Sew them together into a row, pressing the seam allowances in one direction. Repeat to make a second row and press the seam allowances in the opposite direction of the first row. Sew the two rows together to make an appliqué background section measuring 12½" x 48½". Press the seam allowances in one direction. Make two appliqué background sections.

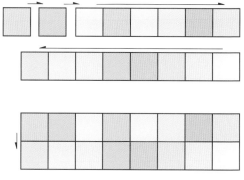

Make 2.

PIECING THE BLOCKS

1. Make a strip set that uses one of each of the brown, red, green, and blue prints and incorporates one 3"-wide strip, one 2"-wide strip, and two 2½"-wide strips. Press the seam allowances in one direction. Make a total of eight strip sets. Crosscut each strip set into four 8½"-wide segments for a total of 32 blocks (2 will be extra).

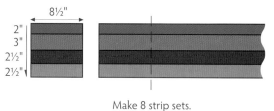

Make 8 strip sets.
Cut 32 segments.

APPLIQUÉING THE BACKGROUND SECTIONS

1. Referring to "Fusible Appliqué" on page 8, use the patterns on pages 23–25 to prepare the following:
   - 2 snowman heads from white flannel
   - 2 hats from black flannel
   - 2 hat bands from red flannel #1
   - 2 scarves from red flannel #1
   - 4 arms from brown flannel (2 of each)
   - 2 noses from orange flannel
   - 6 holly leaves from green flannel
   - 8 stars from gold flannel
   - 1 mitten and 1 reversed from both red flannel #2 and #3
   - 2 mittens and 2 reversed from blue flannel

2. Cut the length of rickrack in half and pin it in place on the appliqué backgrounds. Sew in position, referring to "Using Rickrack" on page 9 for detailed instructions.

3. Using the diagrams below and the photo on page 18 as guides, arrange the appliqué shapes and fuse in place. Appliqué by hand or machine.

Rickrack

Rickrack

Appliqué placement

ASSEMBLING THE QUILT TOP

1. Sew the dark-brown 1" x 42" strips end to end to make one long continuous strip. Crosscut this strip into four strips, 48½" long. Sew one strip to the top and one to the bottom of each appliqué panel. Press the seam allowances toward the dark-brown sashing strips.

2. Arrange the sections of the quilt as shown and sew the sections together. Press the seam allowances toward the dark-brown sashing.

3. Sew the dark-brown 3½" x 42" strips end to end to make one long continuous strip. Crosscut this strip into two strips, 66½" long, and two strips, 54½" long. Sew the 66½"-long strips to the sides of the quilt. Sew the 54½"-long strips to the top and bottom of the quilt. Press the seam allowances toward the dark-brown border.

FINISHING THE QUILT

1. Layer the backing, batting, and quilt top; baste.

2. Quilt as desired. Our quilt is machine quilted with an allover swirl design.

3. Bind the quilt using the dark-brown 2½"-wide strips. Refer to "Binding" on page 11 as needed.

4. Sew on the button accents.

Quilt assembly

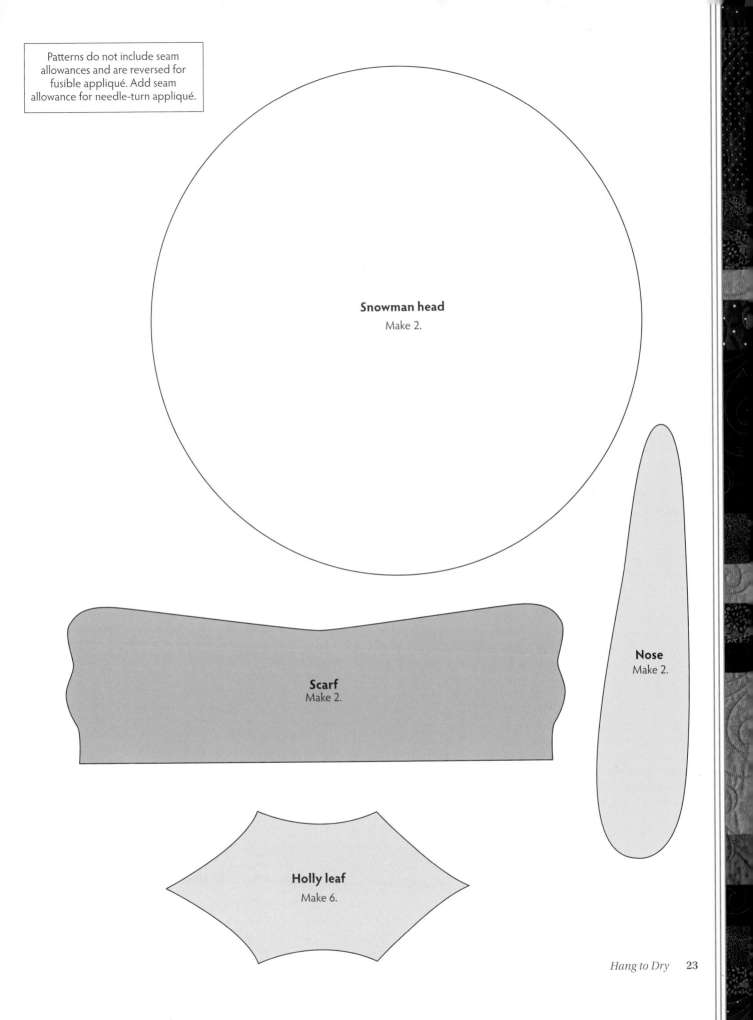

Patterns do not include seam allowances and are reversed for fusible appliqué. Add seam allowance for needle-turn appliqué.

Snowman head
Make 2.

Nose
Make 2.

Scarf
Make 2.

Holly leaf
Make 6.

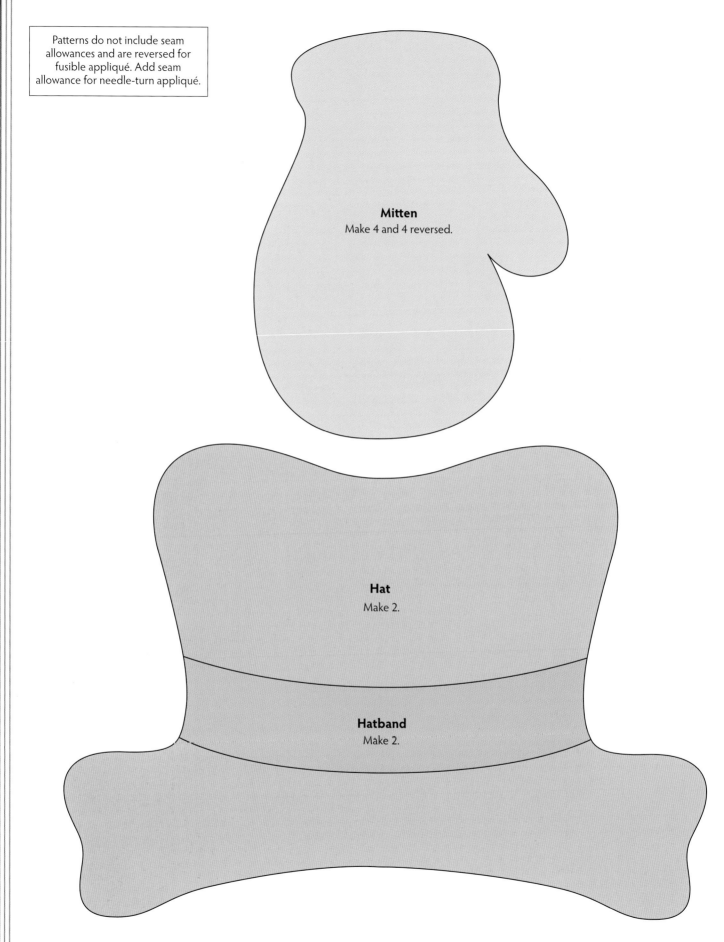

Patterns do not include seam allowances and are reversed for fusible appliqué. Add seam allowance for needle-turn appliqué.

Mitten
Make 4 and 4 reversed.

Hat
Make 2.

Hatband
Make 2.

Patterns do not include seam allowances and are reversed for fusible appliqué. Add seam allowance for needle-turn appliqué.

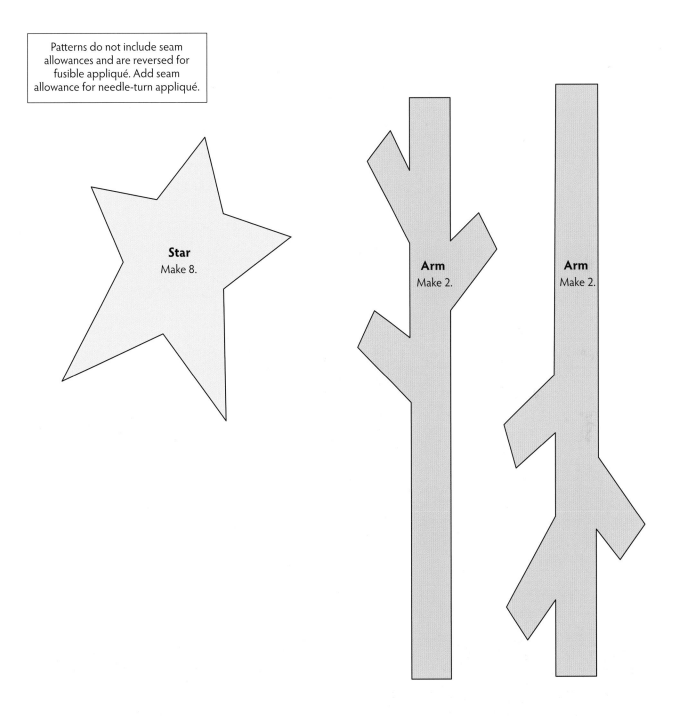

Star
Make 8.

Arm
Make 2.

Arm
Make 2.

Snowstorm Series

A holiday quilt doesn't have to be in traditional red or green colors to add impact to your seasonal decorating. While black may seem like an unusual color choice, we love the stark contrast between the dark background and the appliquéd snowflakes. Also, there's the added benefit of being able to keep it on display longer. If you've ever seen a snowstorm at night, you know it's an amazing sight!

Snowstorm Lap Quilt

FINISHED QUILT: 54½" x 66½"
FINISHED BLOCK: 6" x 6"

MATERIALS

Yardage is based on 42"-wide fabric. Fat quarters measure approximately 18" x 21".

13 fat quarters of assorted black fabrics for blocks
1¼ yards of dark-gray fabric for Nine Patch blocks and binding
⅞ yard of white flannel for snowflakes
3½ yards of fabric for backing
63" x 75" piece of batting
1¼ yards of 18"-wide lightweight fusible web
Matching thread for appliqué

CUTTING

Cut all strips across the width of the fabric.

From *each* of the black fat quarters, cut:
2 strips, 6½" x 21"; crosscut the strips into
    6 squares, 6½" x 6½" (78 total)
1 strip, 2½" x 21" (13 total, 1 is extra)

From the dark-gray fabric, cut:
8 strips, 2½" x 42"; crosscut the strips into
    16 strips, 2½" x 21" (1 is extra)
7 strips, 2½" x 42"

"Snowstorm Lap Quilt," designed and pieced by Jeanne Large and Shelley Wicks, machine quilted by Wendy Findlay.

PIECING THE BLOCKS

1. Sew a dark-gray 2½" x 21" strip to each long side of a black 2½" x 21" strip to make a strip set. Press the seam allowances toward the black strip. Make a total of six strip sets. Crosscut each strip set into seven segments, 2½" wide, for a total of 42 segments.

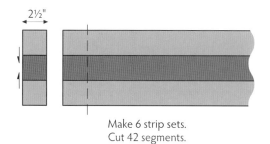

Make 6 strip sets.
Cut 42 segments.

2. Sew a black 2½" x 21" strip to each long side of a dark-gray 2½" x 21" strip to make a strip set. Press the seam allowances toward the black strips. Make a total of three strip sets. Crosscut each strip set into seven segments, 2½" wide, for a total of 21 segments.

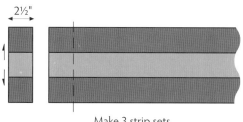

Make 3 strip sets.
Cut 21 segments.

3. Sew a segment from step 1 on each side of a segment from step 2 to make a Nine Patch block. Press the seam allowances toward the center segment. Make 21 Nine Patch blocks.

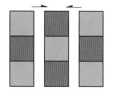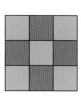

Make 21.

4. Lay out the black 6½" squares and the Nine Patch blocks into 11 rows with nine blocks in each row. Then group and sew the blocks together into sections as shown. This will make it easier to add the appliqués. Press seam allowances in opposite directions from row to row.

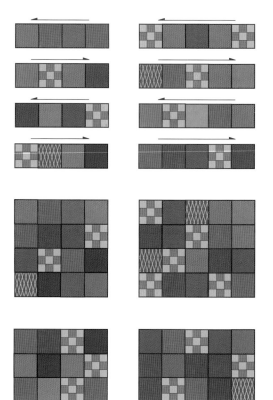

APPLIQUÉING THE QUILT TOP

1. Referring to "Fusible Appliqué" on page 8, use the large snowflake pattern on page 33 to prepare 10 snowflakes from the white flannel.

2. Arrange the snowflakes as shown or as desired, and fuse in place. Using a blanket stitch and white or invisible thread, appliqué the edges by hand or machine.

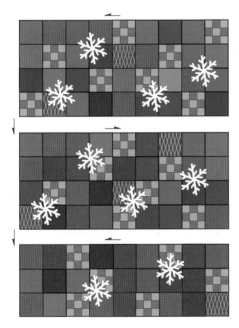

Appliqué placement

ASSEMBLING THE QUILT TOP

Sew the sections together as shown, and then sew the three units together to complete the quilt top. Press the seam allowances as shown.

Quilt assembly

FINISHING THE QUILT

1. Layer the backing, batting, and quilt top; baste.

2. Quilt as desired. Our quilt is machine quilted with an allover design.

3. Bind the quilt using the dark-gray 2½" x 42" strips. Refer to "Binding" on page 11 as needed.

Snowstorm Table Runner

FINISHED RUNNER: 21½" x 45½"
FINISHED BLOCK: 6" x 6"

MATERIALS

Yardage is based on 42"-wide fabric. Fat eighths measure approximately 9" x 21".

1 yard of dark-gray tone on tone for Nine Patch
    blocks, border, and binding

⅜ yard of black tone on tone for Nine Patch
    blocks

4 fat eighths of assorted black prints for
    alternate blocks

¼ yard of white flannel for snowflakes

1⅔ yards of fabric for backing

30" x 59" piece of batting

¾ yard of 18"-wide lightweight fusible web

Matching thread for appliqué

CUTTING

Cut all strips across the width of the fabric.

From the dark-gray tone on tone, cut:
4 strips, 2½" x 42"; crosscut the strips into
    8 strips, 2½" x 21"
4 strips, 2" x 42"
4 strips, 2½" x 42"

From the black tone on tone, cut:
4 strips, 2½" x 42"; crosscut the strips into
    7 strips, 2½" x 21"

From *each* of the black fat eighths, cut:
3 squares, 6½" x 6½" (12 total, 1 is extra)

"Snowstorm Table Runner," designed and pieced by Jeanne Large and Shelley Wicks, machine quilted by Wendy Findlay.

PIECING THE BLOCKS

1. Sew a dark-gray 2½" x 21" strip to each long side of a black 2½" x 21" strip to make a strip set. Press the seam allowances toward the black strip. Make a total of three strip sets. Crosscut the strip sets into 20 segments, 2½" wide.

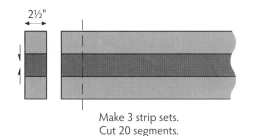

2½"

Make 3 strip sets.
Cut 20 segments.

2. Sew a black 2½" x 21" strip to each long side of a dark-gray 2½" x 21" strip to make a strip set. Press the seam allowances toward the black strips. Make a total of two strip sets. Crosscut the strip sets into 10 segments, 2½" wide.

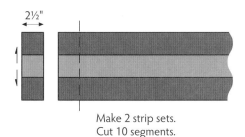

2½"

Make 2 strip sets.
Cut 10 segments.

3. Sew a segment from step 1 on each side of a segment from step 2 to make a Nine Patch block. Press the seam allowances toward the center segment. Make 10 Nine Patch blocks.

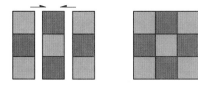

Make 10.

4. Lay out the black 6½" squares and the Nine Patch blocks into three rows with seven blocks in each row. Sew the blocks into rows. Press seam allowances in opposite directions from row to row. Sew the rows together and press the seam allowances in one direction.

5. Sew the dark-gray 2" x 42" strips together end to end and crosscut this strip into two strips, 2" x 42½". Sew one to each long edge of the table runner. Cut two strips, 2" x 21½", and sew one to each end of the table runner. Press the seam allowances toward the border.

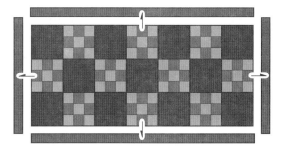

Table-runner assembly

APPLIQUÉING THE TABLE RUNNER

1. Referring to "Fusible Appliqué" on page 8, use the snowflake patterns on page 33 to prepare three large snowflakes and four small snowflakes from the white flannel.

2. Arrange the snowflakes as shown or as desired and fuse in place. Using a blanket stitch and white or invisible thread, appliqué the edges by hand or machine.

FINISHING THE TABLE RUNNER

1. Layer the backing, batting, and table-runner top; baste.

2. Quilt as desired. Our table runner is machine quilted with an allover design.

3. Bind the table runner using the dark-gray 2½" x 42" strips. Refer to "Binding" on page 11 as needed.

Snowstorm Pillow

FINISHED PILLOW: 12" x 12"

MATERIALS

2 pieces of black flannel, 14" x 14", for pillow front and back

2 pieces of muslin, 14" x 14", for layering

1 piece of white flannel, 10" x 10", for snowflake

2 pieces of batting, 14" x 14"

10" x 10" piece of lightweight fusible web

White thread for appliqué

1-pound bag of polyester stuffing

7 ivory buttons, ½" to ¾" diameter

"Snowstorm Pillow," designed and pieced by Jeanne Large and Shelley Wicks, machine quilted by Jeanne Large.

MAKING THE PILLOW

1. Place a square of batting on top of a muslin square. Lay a square of black flannel right side up on top of the batting. Baste the layers together and quilt as desired; we used a stipple design. Repeat with the remaining squares of flannel, batting, and muslin.

2. Trim the two quilted pieces to 12½" x 12½".

3. Referring to "Fusible Appliqué" on page 8, prepare the large snowflake from the white flannel using the pattern on page 33. Center the snowflake on one of the 12½" squares and fuse in place. Using a blanket stitch and white thread, appliqué the edges by hand or machine. Sew the buttons on as shown.

Appliqué and button placement

4. Lay the pillow front and pillow back with right sides together. Sew all around the outer edges, leaving a 4" opening along one side. Turn the pillow right side out. Stuff firmly and hand stitch the opening closed.

Leave a 4" opening for turning.

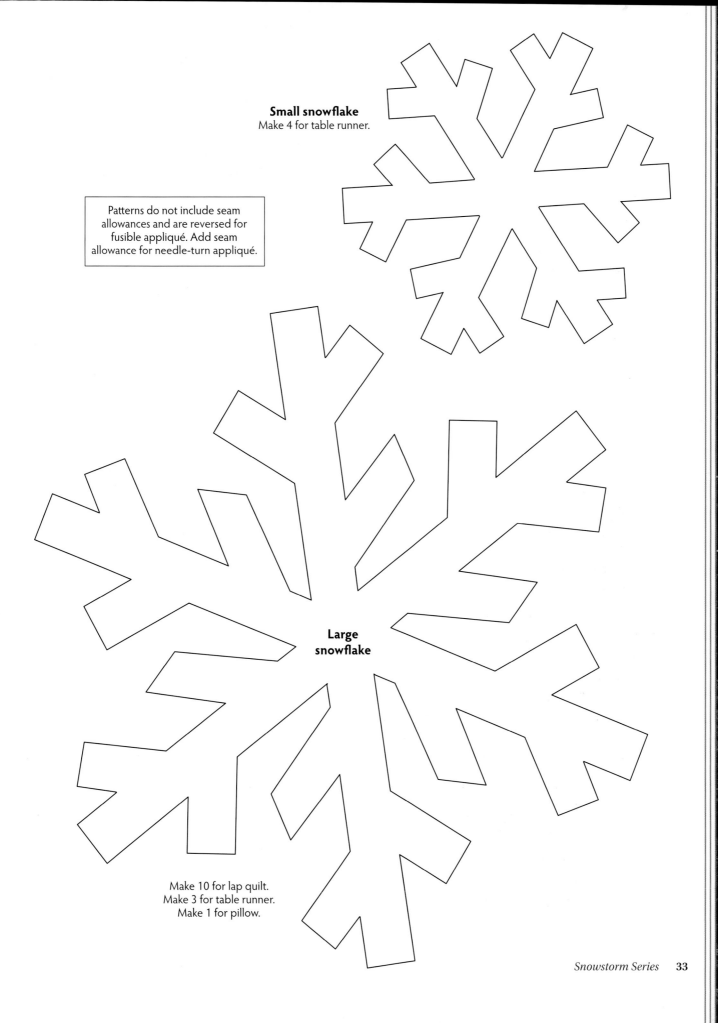

Small snowflake
Make 4 for table runner.

Patterns do not include seam allowances and are reversed for fusible appliqué. Add seam allowance for needle-turn appliqué.

Large snowflake

Make 10 for lap quilt.
Make 3 for table runner.
Make 1 for pillow.

Too Many Trees Set

Celebrate the season with these quirky pine trees. This quilt will add some "light and bright" to any room, all winter long. And really, you can never have too many trees—or quilts, for that matter!

Too Many Trees Lap Quilt

FINISHED QUILT: 59" x 77½"

MATERIALS

Yardage is based on 42"-wide fabric.

3⅝ yards of white solid for blocks and sashing

2⅞ yards of red print for blocks, sashing, and binding

6 pieces of assorted green prints, 12" x 18", for trees

13" x 21" piece of gold print #1 for small stars

10" x 24" piece of gold print #2 for large stars

11" x 20" piece of brown print for tree trunks

4⅞ yards of fabric for backing

67" x 86" piece of batting

3¼ yards of 18"-wide lightweight fusible web

Matching thread for appliqué

CUTTING

Cut all strips across the width of the fabric.

From the white solid, cut:

3 strips, 9" x 42"; crosscut the strips into 12 squares, 9" x 9"

8 strips, 3" x 42"; crosscut the strips into 24 rectangles, 3" x 11"

12 strips, 3" x 42"; crosscut the strips into 24 rectangles, 3" x 16"

20 strips, 1½" x 42"

From the red print, cut:

6 strips, 1½" x 42"; crosscut the strips into 24 strips, 1½" x 9"

8 strips, 1½" x 42"; crosscut the strips into 24 strips, 1½" x 11"

34 strips, 1½" x 42"

7 strips, 2½" x 42"

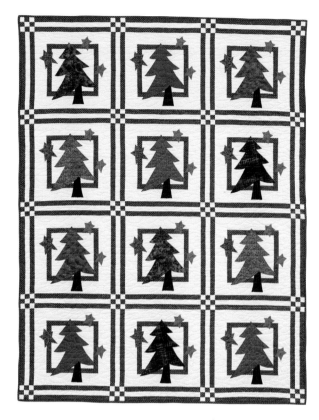

"Too Many Trees Lap Quilt," designed and made by Shelley Wicks and Jeanne Large, machine quilted by Wendy Findlay.

PIECING THE BLOCKS

1. Sew a red 1½" x 9" strip to each side of a white 9" square. Sew red 1½" x 11" strips to the top and bottom of the white square. Press the seam allowances toward the red strips.

2. Sew a white 3" x 11" rectangle to each side of the unit from step 1. Sew white 3" x 16" rectangles to the top and bottom of the unit. Press the seam allowances toward the white rectangles. Make a total of 12 blocks.

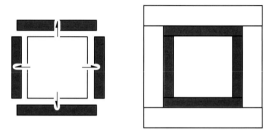

Make 12.

APPLIQUÉING THE BLOCKS

1. Referring to "Fusible Appliqué" on page 8, use the patterns on pages 40 and 41 to prepare the following:

   - 12 trees from green prints
   - 12 tree trunks from brown print
   - 12 large stars from gold print #2
   - 24 small stars from gold print #1

2. Arrange one tree, one large star, and two small stars on each block as shown and fuse in place. Using a blanket stitch and matching thread, appliqué the edges by hand or machine.

Appliqué placement

MAKING THE SASHING

1. Sew a red 1½" x 42" strip to each long side of a white 1½" x 42" strip. Press the seam allowances toward the red strips. Make 16 of these strip sets. Crosscut the strip sets into 31 segments, 16" wide. From the remainder of the strip sets, cut a total of 20 segments, 1½" wide.

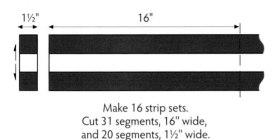

Make 16 strip sets.
Cut 31 segments, 16" wide,
and 20 segments, 1½" wide.

2. Using the remaining white and red 1½" x 42" strips, make two strip sets as shown. Press the seam allowances toward the red strips. Crosscut the strip sets into 40 segments, 1½" wide.

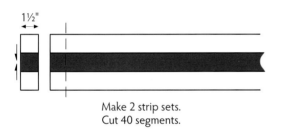

Make 2 strip sets.
Cut 40 segments.

3. Sew two segments from step 2 to a segment from step 1 as shown to make a Nine Patch block. Press the seam allowances toward the center unit. Make 20 Nine Patch blocks.

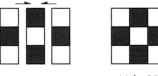

Make 20.

ASSEMBLING THE QUILT TOP

1. Arrange the Tree blocks into four rows of three blocks each. Place a 3½" x 16" strip-set segment between each block, and at each end of the rows. Sew the blocks and sashing strips together into rows. Press the seam allowances toward the sashing strips.

2. Lay out the remaining sashing and Nine Patch blocks as shown. Sew the four Nine Patch blocks and three sashing segments together into a row. Press the seam allowances toward the sashing segments. Make five rows. Sew the block rows and sashing rows together as shown. Press the seam allowances toward the sashing.

Quilt assembly

FINISHING THE QUILT

1. Layer the backing, batting, and quilt top; baste.

2. Quilt as desired. Our quilt is machine quilted with an allover design of trees and stars.

3. Bind the quilt using the red 2½"-wide strips. Refer to "Binding" on page 11 as needed.

"Too Many Trees Pillow," designed and made by Shelley Wicks and Jeanne Large, machine quilted by Jeanne Large.

Too Many Trees Pillow

FINISHED PILLOW: 16" x 16"

MATERIALS

Yardages are based on 42"-wide fabric. Fat quarters measure approximately 18" x 21".

⅝ yard of white tone on tone for pillow front and back

¼ yard of red print for pillow front and binding

1 fat quarter of muslin for layering

11" x 12" piece of green print for tree

5" x 8" piece of gold print #1 for large stars

4" x 9" piece of gold print #2 for small stars

4" x 6" piece of brown print for tree trunk

17" x 17" piece of batting

½ yard of 18"-wide lightweight fusible web

Matching thread for appliqué

16" square pillow form

8 red buttons, ¼" to ¾" diameter

CUTTING

Cut all strips across the width of the fabric.

From the white tone on tone, cut:

1 square, 9" x 9"

2 rectangles, 3" x 11"

2 rectangles, 3" x 16"

1 strip, 11" x 42"; crosscut the strip into
2 rectangles, 11" x 16"

From the red print, cut:

1 strip, 1½" x 42"; crosscut the strip into:
2 strips, 1½" x 9"
2 strips, 1½" x 11"

2 strips, 2½" x 42"

From the muslin, cut:

1 square, 17" x 17"

MAKING THE PILLOW TOP

1. Sew a red 1½" x 9" strip to each side of the white 9" square. Sew the red 1½" x 11" strips to the top and bottom of the white square. Press the seam allowances toward the red strips.

2. Sew a white 3" x 11" rectangle to each side of the unit from step 1. Sew the white 3" x 16" rectangles to the top and bottom of the unit. Press the seam allowances toward the red strips.

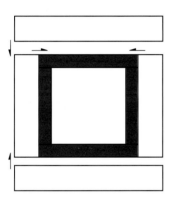

3. Layer the muslin backing square, batting, and pillow top; baste.

4. Quilt as desired. Our pillow is quilted in an allover design of loops.

APPLIQUÉING THE PILLOW TOP

1. Referring to "Fusible Appliqué" on page 8, use the patterns on pages 40 and 41 to prepare the following:
   - 1 tree from green print
   - 2 large stars from gold print #1
   - 3 small stars from gold print #2
   - 1 tree trunk from brown print

2. Arrange the tree and stars on the pillow top as shown and fuse in place. Using a blanket stitch and matching thread, appliqué the edges by hand or machine.

Appliqué placement

FINISHING THE PILLOW

1. Sew the buttons on the tree as desired, or refer to the photograph on page 38 for placement guidance.

2. To make the pillow backing, turn under ½" of one long side of each white 11" x 16" backing rectangle. Stitch ¼" from the fold. Lay the backing pieces under the pillow top, with both wrong sides facing the wrong side of the pillow top and outer edges even with the pillow top. The hemmed edges will overlap in the center of the pillow. Sew all around the outer edges of the pillow using a ¼" seam allowance.

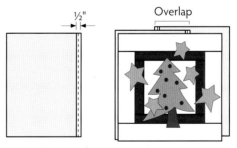

Make 2.

3. Bind the pillow using the red 2½"-wide strips, referring to "Binding" on page 11 as needed. Insert the pillow form through the opening in the back.

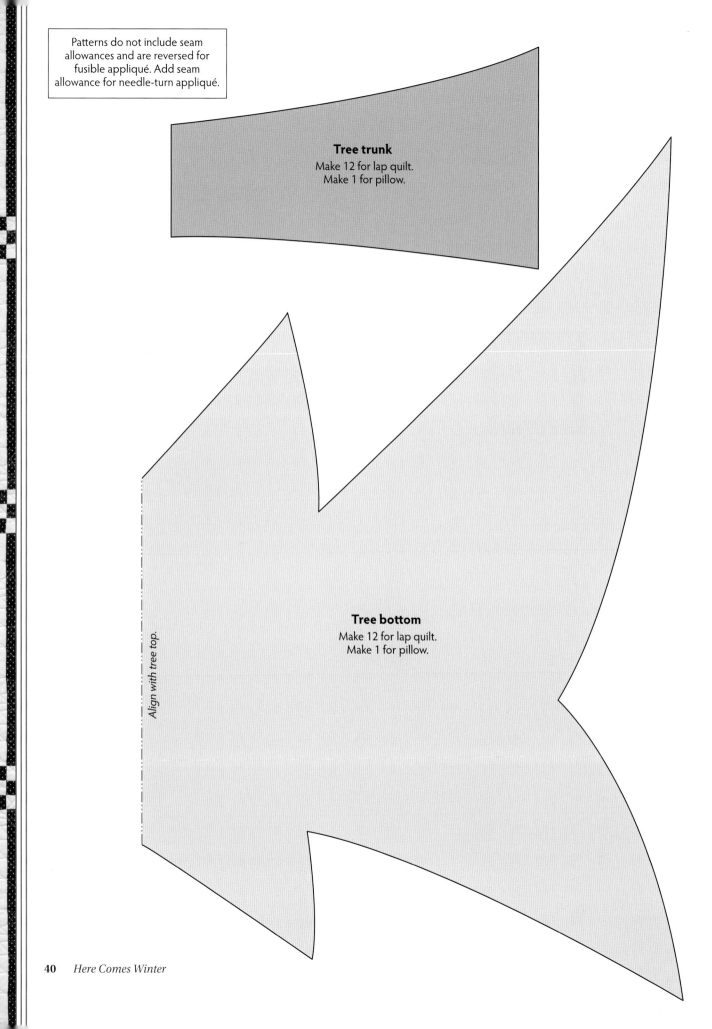

Patterns do not include seam allowances and are reversed for fusible appliqué. Add seam allowance for needle-turn appliqué.

Tree trunk
Make 12 for lap quilt.
Make 1 for pillow.

Align with tree top.

Tree bottom
Make 12 for lap quilt.
Make 1 for pillow.

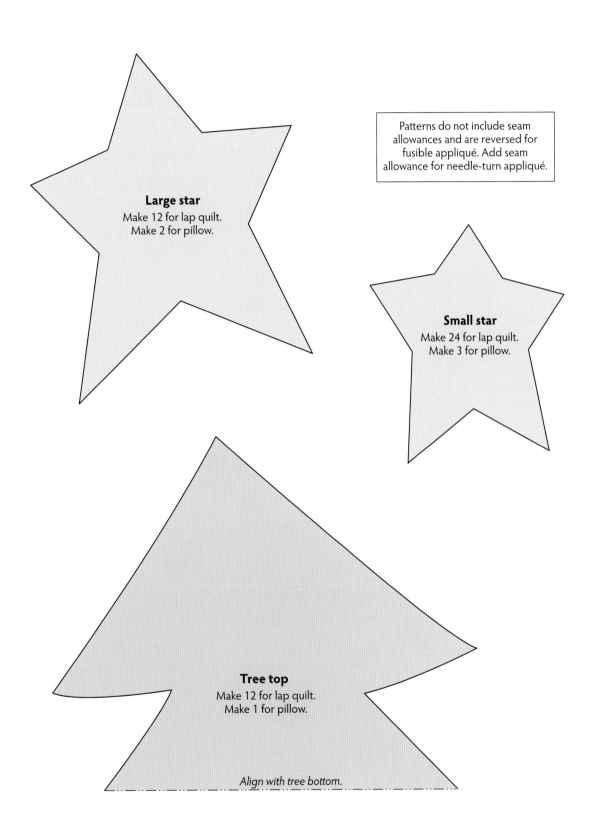

Large star
Make 12 for lap quilt.
Make 2 for pillow.

Patterns do not include seam
allowances and are reversed for
fusible appliqué. Add seam
allowance for needle-turn appliqué.

Small star
Make 24 for lap quilt.
Make 3 for pillow.

Tree top
Make 12 for lap quilt.
Make 1 for pillow.

Align with tree bottom.

"Hot Toddy," designed and pieced by Jeanne Large and Shelley Wicks, machine quilted by Wendy Findlay.

Hot Toddy

Snuggle under this quilt with a hot toddy and a good book. What a great way to spend a cold winter day!

FINISHED QUILT: 75½" x 93½" • FINISHED BLOCK: 18" x 18"

MATERIALS

Yardages are based on 42"-wide fabric. Fat quarters measure approximately 18" x 21".

3½ yards of black tone on tone for blocks, borders, and binding

1⅞ yards of green print #1 for star backgrounds and pieced border

1 yard of green print #2 for star backgrounds

½ yard of red tone on tone for pieced border

½ yard of beige print for blocks

⅜ yard *each* of 4 red prints for star points

1 fat quarter *each* of 3 gold prints for pinwheels

5⅔ yards of fabric for backing

84" x 102" piece of batting

Accuracy Matters

Accurate cutting and piecing are very important for this quilt. Press seam allowances open to alleviate the bulk where multiple points meet. Spray your finished block with spray starch to help keep the block flat and square.

CUTTING

Cut all strips across the width of the fabric. Be sure to label the triangles with their size as you cut them and keep like triangles together.

From the black tone on tone, cut:

4 strips, 5⅜" x 42"; crosscut the strips into 24 squares, 5⅜" x 5⅜". Cut each square in half diagonally to yield 48 triangles.

2 strips, 5¾" x 42"; crosscut the strips into 12 squares, 5¾" x 5¾". Cut each square into quarters diagonally to yield 48 triangles.

1 strip, 5" x 42"; crosscut the strip into 4 squares, 5" x 5"

8 strips, 6½" x 42"

9 strips, 2½" x 42"

From the beige print, cut:

2 strips, 5¾" x 42"; crosscut the strips into 12 squares, 5¾" x 5¾". Cut each square into quarters diagonally to yield 48 triangles.

From *each* of the gold fat quarters, cut:

3 strips, 5⅜" x 21"; crosscut the strips into 8 squares, 5⅜" x 5⅜" (24 total). Cut each square in half diagonally to yield 16 triangles (48 total).

From *each* of the red prints, cut:

2 strips, 5⅜" x 42"; crosscut the strips into 12 squares, 5⅜" x 5⅜" (48 total). Cut each square in half diagonally to yield 24 triangles (96 total).

Continued on page 44

Continued from page 43

From green print #1, cut:

2 strips, 10¼" x 42"; crosscut the strips into 6 squares, 10¼" x 10¼". Cut each square into quarters diagonally to yield 24 triangles.

2 strips, 5⅜" x 42"; crosscut the strips into 12 squares, 5⅜" x 5⅜". Cut each square in half diagonally to yield 24 triangles.

14 strips, 2" x 42"

From green print #2, cut:

2 strips, 10¼" x 42"; crosscut the strips into 6 squares, 10¼" x 10¼". Cut each square into quarters diagonally to yield 24 triangles.

2 strips, 5⅜" x 42"; crosscut the strips into 12 squares, 5⅜" x 5⅜". Cut each square in half diagonally to yield 24 triangles.

From the red tone on tone, cut:

7 strips, 2" x 42"

PIECING THE BLOCKS

1. Sew a black 5¾" triangle to a beige 5¾" triangle as shown. Press the seam allowances toward the black triangle. Sew a gold 5⅜" triangle to the long edge of the unit as shown. Press the seam allowances toward the gold triangle. Make 48 units.

Make 48.

2. Arrange four matching units from step 1 to form a Pinwheel block. Sew the units together into rows. Press the seam allowances open. Sew the rows together, and press the seam allowances open. Make 12 Pinwheel blocks.

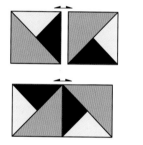
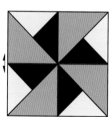

Make 12.

3. Arrange two matching red 5⅜" triangles on each short side of a green 10¼" triangle. Sew the triangles together to make a star-point unit. Press the seam allowances toward the red triangles. Repeat to make 48 star-point units.

Make 48.

4. Sew a green 5⅜" triangle and a black 5⅜" triangle together to make a half-square-triangle unit. Press the seam allowances

toward the black triangles. Make 48 half-square-triangle units.

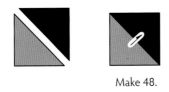

Make 48.

5. Arrange the star-point units and half-square-triangle units with a Pinwheel block as shown, using matching backgrounds and corner units. Sew the units together in vertical rows and press the seam allowances open. Sew the rows together and press the seam allowances open. Make 12 blocks.

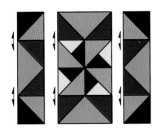 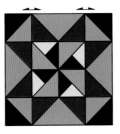

Make 12.

ASSEMBLING THE QUILT TOP

1. Arrange the blocks into four rows of three blocks each. Sew the blocks together into rows. Press the seam allowances open. Sew the rows together and press the seam allowances open.

2. Sew a red 2" x 42" strip between two green 2" x 42" strips. Press the seam allowances toward the red strip. Repeat to make seven strip sets.

Make 7.

3. Trim the ends of each strip set so they are straight and sew them end to end to make one long continuous strip. From this strip cut two strips, 72½" long, and two strips, 54½" long.

4. Sew a 72½"-long strip to each side of the quilt. Press the seam allowances toward the pieced strips. Sew a black 5" square to each end of the 54½"-long strips. Press the seam allowances toward the strips. Sew these strips to the top and bottom of the quilt top. Press the seam allowances toward the pieced strips.

5. Sew the black 6½"-wide strips end to end to make one continuous strip. From this strip cut two strips, 6½" x 81½", and 2 strips, 6½" x 75½". Sew the 81½"-long strips to the sides of the quilt. Sew the 75½"-long strips to the top and bottom of the quilt top. Press the seam allowances toward the black border.

Quilt assembly

FINISHING THE QUILT

1. Layer the backing, batting, and quilt top; baste.

2. Quilt as desired. Our quilt is machine quilted with an allover design.

3. Bind the quilt using the black 2½"-wide strips. Refer to "Binding" on page 11 as needed.

Run, Run, Rudolph Pair

Fun and frolic make this festive pair of projects a hit! Over the rooftops and through the starry sky, these reindeer are on their way to your house. Use the lap quilt on your sofa and place the coordinating table topper nearby.

Run, Run, Rudolph Lap Quilt

FINISHED QUILT: 52½" x 56½"

MATERIALS

Yardage is based on 42"-wide fabric. Fat quarters measure approximately 18" x 21" and fat eighths measure approximately 9" x 21".

1¾ yards of gold print for sashing, borders, and binding

1 fat quarter of black print for center panel

4 fat eighths of assorted medium-beige prints for checkerboard border

4 fat eighths of assorted dark-beige prints for checkerboard border

4 fat eighths of assorted red prints for pieced border

4 fat eighths of assorted green prints for pieced border

3 fat eighths of assorted gold prints for pieced border

1 fat eighth of dark-brown print for reindeer

10" x 11" piece of green plaid for trees

7" x 12" piece of gold print for stars

6" x 11" piece of red print for house

6" x 6" piece of gold print for roof

4" x 5" piece of red print for harnesses

3" x 4" piece of white print for windows

2" x 5" piece of light-brown print for door

3" x 3" piece of brown print for tree trunks

3½ yards of fabric for backing

60" x 64" piece of batting

1¼ yards of 18"-wide lightweight fusible web

Dark-charcoal thread for appliqué

CUTTING

Cut all strips across the width of the fabric.

From the black fat quarter, cut:
1 rectangle, 14½" x 18½"

From the gold print, cut:
2 strips, 1½" x 42"; crosscut the strips into:
    2 strips, 1½" x 18½"
    2 strips, 1½" x 16½"
10 strips, 2½" x 42"; trim *4 of the strips* to
    2½" x 32½"
6 strips, 4½" x 42"

From *each* of the medium- and dark-beige fat eighths, cut:
3 strips, 2½" x 21" (24 total)

From *each* of the red, green, and gold fat eighths, cut:
2 strips, 3½" x 21" (22 total); crosscut the strips into 8 rectangles, 3½" x 4½" (88 total, 4 are extra)

"Run, Run, Rudolph Lap Quilt," designed and made by Shelley Wicks and Jeanne Large, machine quilted by Wendy Findlay.

PIECING THE QUILT TOP

1. Sew a gold 1½" x 18½" strip to each long side of the black rectangle. Sew gold 1½" x 16½" strips to the top and bottom of the rectangle. Press the seam allowances toward the black rectangle.

2. Sew a dark-beige 2½" x 21" strip to each long side of a medium-beige 2½" x 21" strip. Press the seam allowances toward the dark-beige strips. Make four strip sets. Crosscut the strip sets into 24 segments, 2½" wide.

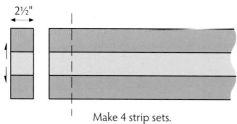

2½"

Make 4 strip sets.
Cut 24 segments.

3. Sew a medium-beige 2½" x 21" strip to each long side of a dark-beige 2½" x 21" strip. Press the seam allowances toward the dark-beige strip. Make four strip sets. Crosscut the strip sets into 24 segments, 2½" wide.

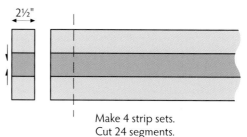

2½"

Make 4 strip sets.
Cut 24 segments.

4. Sew 10 segments together, alternating the segments from steps 2 and 3 to make a checkerboard section. Make two sections. Press the seam allowances to one side. Sew one section to each side of the center rectangle as shown, having a dark/medium/dark segment at the top on one side and at the bottom on the opposite side. Press the seam allowances toward the gold sashing.

Dark/medium/dark
at the top

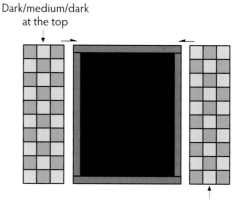

Dark/medium/dark
at the bottom

5. Sew 14 segments from steps 2 and 3 together, alternating them as before. Make two sections. Press the seam allowances to one side. Sew one section to the top and one to the bottom of the center rectangle as shown, maintaining the checkerboard pattern. Press the seam allowances toward the gold sashing.

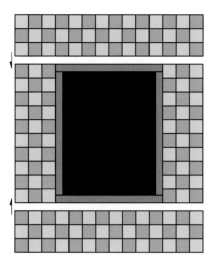

6. Sew a gold 2½" x 32½" strip to each side of the quilt. Sew the remaining gold 2½" x 32½" strips to the top and bottom. Press the seam allowances toward the gold border.

APPLIQUÉING THE QUILT TOP

1. Referring to "Fusible Appliqué" on page 8, use the patterns on pages 55–57 to prepare the following:
   - 3 reindeer from dark-brown print
   - 3 harnesses from red print
   - 2 large trees from green plaid
   - 2 tree trunks from brown print
   - 1 house from red print
   - 1 roof from gold print
   - 2 windows from white print
   - 1 door from light-brown print
   - 6 small stars from gold print

2. Arrange the shapes as shown and fuse in place. Using a blanket stitch and dark-charcoal thread, appliqué the edges by hand or machine. Stitch by hand, use machine embroidery, or free-motion quilt to make the reindeer antlers and eyes.

Appliqué placement

ADDING THE BORDERS

1. Sew the red, green, and gold rectangles together randomly in pairs, along the 4½" edges. Press the seam allowances to one side. Make 34 pairs.

2. Sew nine pairs together along the 6½" edges to make a section 6½" x 36½". Press the seam allowances in one direction. Make two sections and sew them to opposite sides of the quilt. Press the seam allowances toward the gold border.

3. In the same way, sew eight pairs together to make a section measuring 6½" x 32½". Press seam allowances in one direction. Make two sections.

4. Cut 16 of the remaining 3½" x 4½" rectangles to measure 3½" x 3½". Sew the squares randomly into pairs and press the seam allowances to one side. Sew two pairs together to make a Four Patch block. Press the seam allowances to one side. Make four Four Patch blocks. Sew one to each end of the sections from step 3. Sew one section to the top and one to the bottom of the quilt. Press the seam allowances toward the gold border.

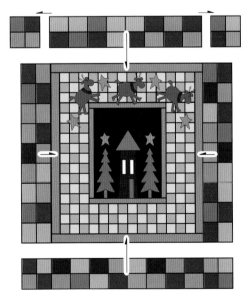

5. Sew the gold 4½"-wide strips end to end to make one long continuous strip. From this strip cut two strips, 4½" x 48½", and two strips, 4½" x 52½". Sew a 48½"-long strip to each side of the quilt. Sew the 52½"-long strips to the top and bottom of the quilt. Press the seam allowances toward the gold border.

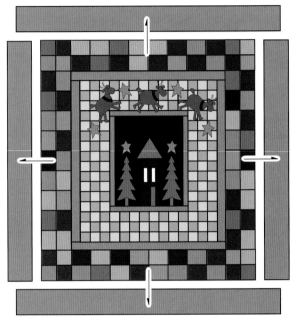

Quilt assembly

FINISHING THE QUILT

1. Layer the backing, batting, and quilt top; baste.

2. Quilt as desired. Our quilt is machine quilted with an allover design of stars and loops.

3. Bind the quilt using the remaining gold 2½"-wide strips. Refer to "Binding" on page 11 as needed.

Run, Run, Rudolph Table Topper

FINISHED QUILT: 44½" x 44½"

MATERIALS

Yardage is based on 42"-wide fabric.
Fat eighths measure approximately 9" x 21".

⅞ yard of red tone on tone for outer border
and binding

6 fat eighths of assorted light-beige prints for
checkerboard border

6 fat eighths of assorted medium-beige prints
for checkerboard border

3 fat eighths of assorted red prints for quilt
center

3 fat eighths of assorted green prints for quilt
center

2 fat eighths of assorted gold prints for quilt
center

14" x 18" piece of dark-brown print for
reindeer

10" x 10" piece of gold print for stars

9" x 9" piece *each* of 2 green prints for trees

4" x 7" piece of red print for reindeer
harnesses

3 yards of fabric for backing

52" x 52" piece of batting

3½ yards of 1½"-wide gold rickrack

3½ yards of ½"-wide gold rickrack

1 yard of 18"-wide lightweight fusible web

Matching thread for appliqué

CUTTING

Cut all strips across the width of the fabric.

**From *each* of the red, green, and gold fat
eighths, cut:**
2 strips, 4" x 21"; crosscut the strips into
  8 squares, 4" x 4" (64 total)

**From *each* of the light- and medium-beige
fat eighths, cut:**
3 strips, 2½" x 21" (36 total)

From the red tone on tone, cut:
10 strips, 2½" x 42"

*"Run, Run, Rudolph Table Topper," designed and made by Shelley
Wicks and Jeanne Large, machine quilted by Wendy Findlay.*

PIECING THE QUILT CENTER

1. Lay out the 64 red, green, and gold 4" squares into eight rows, with eight squares in each row. Sew the squares together into rows, pressing the seam allowances in opposite directions from row to row. Sew the rows together, pressing the seam allowances in one direction.

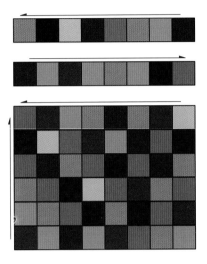

2. Place the 1½"-wide gold rickrack along the raw edge of the quilt center. Line up the rickrack so the inner curve of the rickrack is aligned with the outer edge of the quilt and the outer curve is off the quilt. Pin in place and sew using a small zigzag stitch, keeping one edge of the stitch along the outer edge of the quilt. Repeat on each side of the quilt. Using a rotary cutter and ruler, trim the excess rickrack on all sides of the quilt.

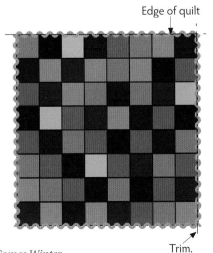

Edge of quilt

Trim.

ADDING THE CHECKERBOARD BORDER

1. Sew a light-beige 2½" x 21" strip to each long edge of a medium-beige 2½" x 21" strip. Press the seam allowances toward the medium-beige strip. Make six strip sets. Crosscut the strip sets into 34 segments, 2½" wide.

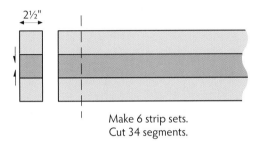

2½"

Make 6 strip sets.
Cut 34 segments.

2. Sew a medium-beige 2½" x 21" strip to each long edge of a light-beige 2½" x 21" strip. Press the seam allowances toward the medium-beige strips. Make six strip sets. Crosscut the strip sets into 34 segments, 2½" wide.

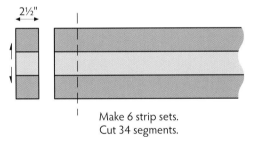

2½"

Make 6 strip sets.
Cut 34 segments.

3. Sew 14 segments together, alternating the segments from steps 1 and 2 to make a checkerboard section. Press the seam allowances to one side. Make two. Sew a section to each side of the quilt center as shown, having a medium/light/medium segment at the bottom on one side and at

the top on the opposite side. Press the seam allowances toward the checkerboard border.

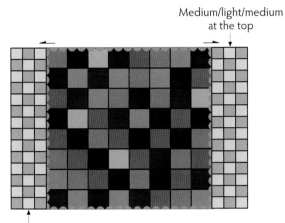

Medium/light/medium at the top

Medium/light/medium at the bottom

4. Sew 20 segments from steps 1 and 2 together, alternating them as before. Press the seam allowances to one side. Make two sections. Sew one section to the top and one to the bottom of the quilt center, maintaining the checkerboard pattern. Press the seam allowances toward the checkerboard border.

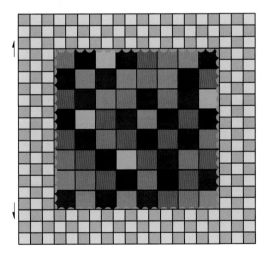

5. Sew ⅛" inside the raw edges all around the quilt. This will secure the seams while you do the appliqué.

APPLIQUÉING THE QUILT

1. Referring to "Fusible Appliqué" on page 8, use the patterns on pages 56 and 57 to prepare the following:
   ◆ 4 reindeer from dark-brown print
   ◆ 4 harnesses from red print
   ◆ 8 small trees from green prints
   ◆ 4 large stars from gold print

2. Arrange the ½"-wide gold rickrack in the borders as shown below and pin in place. Referring to "Using Rickrack" on page 9, sew the rickrack to the quilt top.

3. Arrange the appliqué shapes and fuse in place. Using a blanket stitch and matching thread, appliqué the edges by hand or machine.

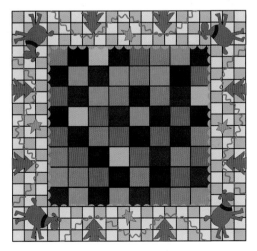

Appliqué placement

ADDING THE OUTER BORDER

1. Sew three of the red 2½" x 42" strips together end to end to make one long continuous strip. From this cut two strips, 2½" x 44½". From two red 2½" x 42" strips, cut two strips, 2½" x 40½".

2. Sew the 40½"-long strips to the sides of the quilt. Sew the 44½"-long strips to the top and bottom of the quilt. Press the seam allowances toward the red border.

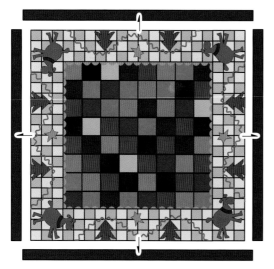

Table-topper assembly

3. Machine embroider the reindeer's antlers and eyes in the color of your choice, referring to "Machine Embroidery" on page 9 for detailed instructions.

FINISHING THE QUILT

1. Layer the backing, batting, and quilt top. Baste.

2. Quilt as desired. Our quilt is custom quilted in a meandering pattern.

3. Bind the quilt using the remaining red 2½"-wide strips. Refer to "Binding" on page 11 as needed.

Make It a Tree Skirt!

Need a tree skirt? Here's an easy way to transform this fun piece into a tree skirt. The only difference in the materials list is extra fabric for additional binding. Instead of ⅞ yard of fabric for the border and binding, you will need 1⅝ yards to allow for bias binding.

1. After the quilt is quilted, but before attaching the binding, draw an 8"-diameter circle in the center of the quilt. Using a sharp pair of scissors, cut out the circle directly on the drawn line.

2. Using a ruler and rotary cutter, carefully cut a straight line from the center of one side of the quilt to the cutout circle.

3. Refer to "Bias Binding" on page 12 for instructions on cutting fabric on the bias. You will need approximately 260" of bias binding to bind the tree skirt.

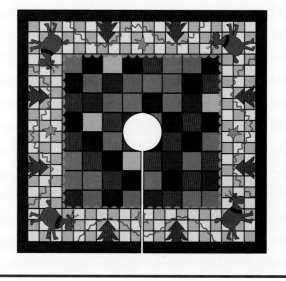

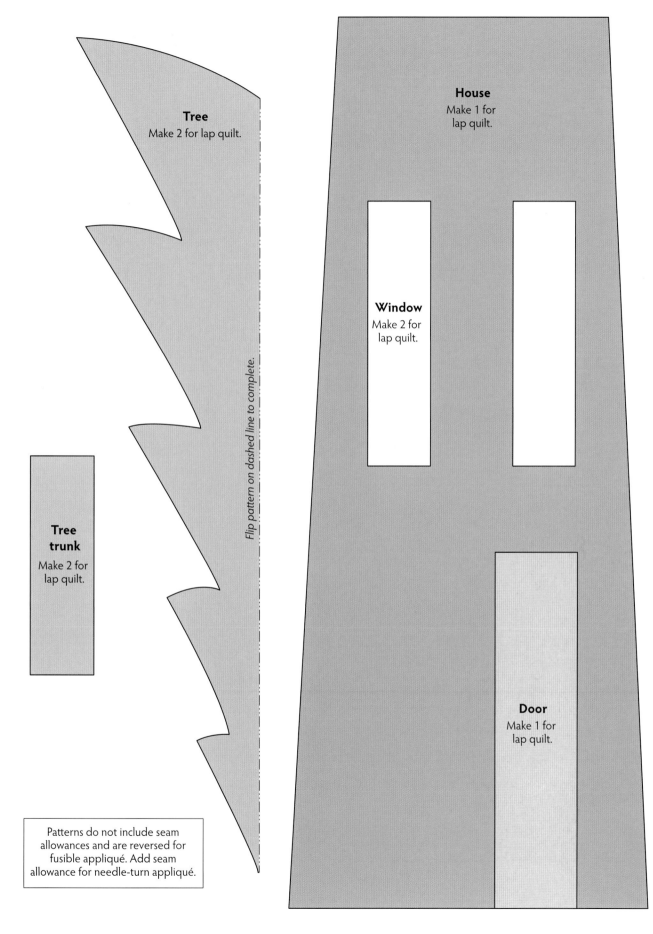

Tree
Make 2 for lap quilt.

Flip pattern on dashed line to complete.

Tree trunk
Make 2 for lap quilt.

House
Make 1 for lap quilt.

Window
Make 2 for lap quilt.

Door
Make 1 for lap quilt.

Patterns do not include seam allowances and are reversed for fusible appliqué. Add seam allowance for needle-turn appliqué.

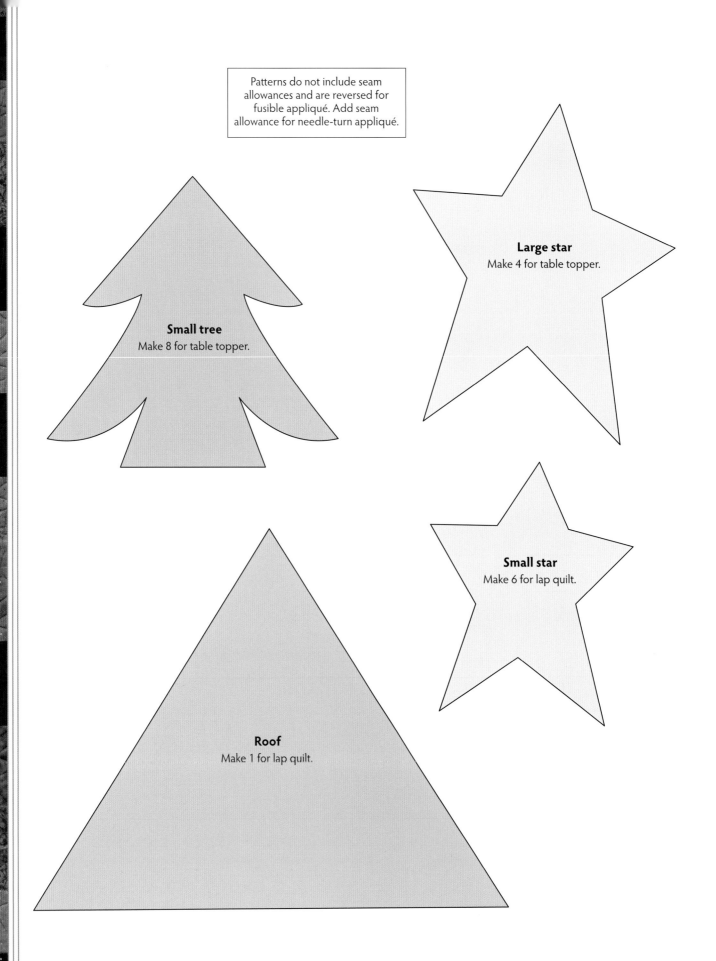

Patterns do not include seam allowances and are reversed for fusible appliqué. Add seam allowance for needle-turn appliqué.

Large star
Make 4 for table topper.

Small tree
Make 8 for table topper.

Small star
Make 6 for lap quilt.

Roof
Make 1 for lap quilt.

Patterns do not include seam allowances and are reversed for fusible appliqué. Add seam allowance for needle-turn appliqué.

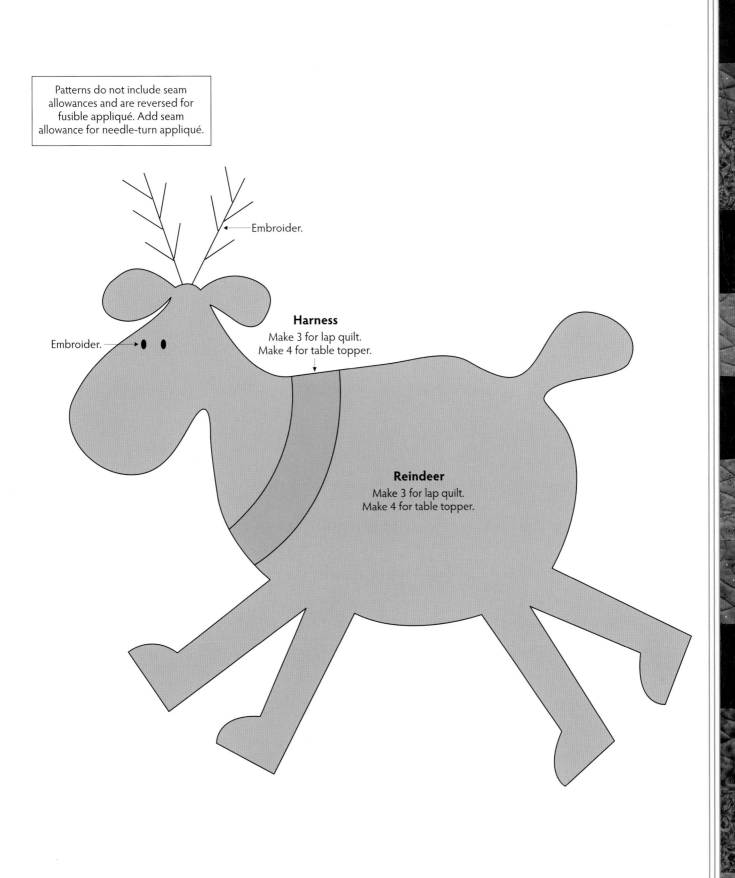

Embroider.

Embroider.

Harness
Make 3 for lap quilt.
Make 4 for table topper.

Reindeer
Make 3 for lap quilt.
Make 4 for table topper.

A Few Good Men Group

Nothing says winter like a perky snowman—or better yet, four or even eight! Whether you have snow in your neck of the woods or hot weather all year round, this cute quilt will warm the hearts and souls of those around you. The banner of stacked snowmen will add charm to any small nook in your house.

A Few Good Men Lap Quilt

FINISHED QUILT: 55½" x 59½"
FINISHED SNOWMAN BLOCK: 10" x 12"
FINISHED SNOWFLAKE BLOCK: 10" x 10"

MATERIALS

Yardage is based on 42"-wide fabric.

3⅛ yards of dark-brown flannel for appliqué backgrounds, first border, fourth border, and binding

⅝ yard of red flannel for checkerboard blocks and second border

⅝ yard of green flannel for checkerboard blocks and third border

⅝ yard of white flannel for snowmen and snowflakes

7" x 26" piece of gold flannel for stars

10" x 15" piece of medium-brown flannel for arms

6" x 8" piece of orange flannel for noses

5" x 8" piece of green flannel for scarves

5" x 8" piece of red flannel for scarves

3⅝ yards of fabric for backing

64" x 68" piece of batting

2 yards of 18"-wide lightweight fusible web

Matching thread for appliqué

16 black buttons, ¼" diameter

8 red buttons, ½" to ⅝" diameter

8 green buttons, ½" to ⅝" diameter

Black embroidery floss

CUTTING

Cut all strips across the width of the fabric.

From the dark-brown flannel, cut:
5 strips, 10½" x 42"; crosscut the strips into:
   8 rectangles, 10½" x 12½"
   8 rectangles, 6½" x 10½"
5 strips, 2" x 42"
6 strips, 3½" x 42"
6 strips, 2½" x 42"

From the red flannel, cut:
3 strips, 2½" x 42"
5 strips, 2" x 42"

From the green flannel, cut:
3 strips, 2½" x 42"
6 strips, 2" x 42"

"A Few Good Men Lap Quilt," designed and pieced by Shelley Wicks and Jeanne Large, machine quilted by Wendy Findlay.

APPLIQUÉING THE BLOCKS

1. Referring to "Fusible Appliqué" on page 8, use the patterns on pages 65 and 66 to prepare the following:

   ◆ 8 snowmen from white flannel

   ◆ 8 snowflakes from white flannel

   ◆ 16 arms (8 of each) from medium-brown flannel

   ◆ 16 large stars from gold flannel

   ◆ 8 noses from orange flannel

   ◆ 4 scarves from red flannel

   ◆ 4 scarves from green flannel

2. Arrange one snowman shape onto a dark-brown 10½" x 12½" rectangle as shown and fuse in place. Add the arms, scarf, and nose. Using a blanket stitch and matching thread, appliqué the edges by hand or machine. Make eight Snowman blocks.

Make 8.

3. Referring to "Hand Embroidery" on page 9, hand stitch mouths on the snowmen using a running stitch.

4. Arrange a snowflake and two stars onto a dark-brown 6½" x 10½" rectangle as shown and fuse in place. Using a blanket stitch and matching thread, appliqué the edges by hand or machine. Make eight snowflake units.

Make 8.

PIECING THE BLOCKS

1. Sew a red 2½" x 42" strip to the long side of a green 2½" x 42" strip. Press the seam allowances toward the green strip. Make a total of three strip sets. Crosscut the strip sets into 32 segments, 3" wide.

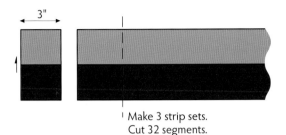

Make 3 strip sets.
Cut 32 segments.

2. Arrange four of the segments, rotating them to form a checkerboard as shown. Sew the segments together to make a unit measuring 4½" x 10½". Make a total of eight checkerboard units. Press the seam allowances in one direction.

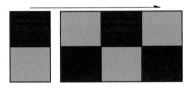

Make 8.

3. Sew a checkerboard unit to one side of a snowflake rectangle. Press the seam allowances toward the snowflake rectangle. Make eight Snowflake blocks.

Make 8.

ASSEMBLING THE QUILT TOP

1. Arrange the Snowman blocks and the Snowflake blocks into four vertical rows of four blocks each, alternating the blocks in each row as shown. Sew the blocks together into rows. Press the seam allowances toward the Snowman blocks. Sew the rows together and press the seam allowances in one direction.

2. Sew the dark-brown 2" x 42" strips end to end to make one long continuous strip. From this strip, cut two strips, 2" x 44½", and two strips, 2" x 43½". Sew the 44½"-long strips to the sides of the quilt. Sew the 43½"-long strips to the top and bottom of the quilt. Press the seam allowances toward the dark-brown border.

3. Sew the red 2" x 42" strips end to end to make one long continuous strip. From this strip, cut two strips, 2" x 47½", and two strips, 2" x 46½". Sew the 47½"-long strips to the sides of the quilt. Sew the 46½"-long strips to the top and bottom of the quilt. Press the seam allowances toward the red border.

4. Sew the green 2" x 42" strips end to end to make one long continuous strip. From this strip, cut two strips, 2" x 50½", and two strips, 2" x 49½". Sew the 50½"-long strips to the sides of the quilt. Sew the 49½"-long strips to the top and bottom of the quilt. Press the seam allowances toward the green border.

5. Sew the dark-brown 3½" x 42" strips end to end to make one long continuous strip. From this strip, cut two strips, 3½" x 53½", and two strips, 3½" x 55½". Sew the 53½"-long strips to the sides of the quilt. Sew the 55½"-long strips to the top and bottom of the quilt. Press the seam allowances toward the dark-brown border.

Quilt assembly

FINISHING THE QUILT

1. Layer the backing, batting, and quilt top; baste.

2. Quilt as desired. Our quilt is machine quilted with an allover design of whimsical stars and swirls.

3. Bind the quilt using the dark-brown 2½"-wide strips. Refer to "Binding" on page 11 as needed.

4. Sew the black buttons on for eyes, and sew the red and green buttons on the snowmen.

A Few Good Men Banner

FINISHED BANNER: 12" x 50"

MATERIALS

Yardage is based on 42"-wide fabric.

1⅝ yards of dark-brown tone on tone for
    background, binding, and backing
12" x 26" piece of white flannel for snowmen
8" x 10" piece of medium-brown print for arms
4" x 18" piece of gold flannel for stars
2" x 22" piece of red flannel for scarves and
    hatband
6" x 6" piece of brown-check flannel for hat
4" x 6" piece of orange flannel for noses
20" x 58" piece of batting
1⅝ yards of ½"-wide gold rickrack
1 yard of 18"-wide lightweight fusible web
Matching thread for appliqué
8 black buttons, ¼" diameter
4 red buttons, ⅝" diameter
12 gold buttons, ½" to ⅝" diameter
Black embroidery floss

CUTTING

**From the dark-brown tone on tone, cut *on
the lengthwise grain*:**
1 strip, 12" x 50"
3 strips, 2½" x length of fabric

From the remaining dark-brown fabric, cut:
1 strip, 20" x 58"

"A Few Good Men Banner," designed and made by Shelley Wicks
and Jeanne Large, machine quilted by Jeanne Large.

and fuse in place. Using a blanket stitch and matching thread, appliqué the edges by hand or machine.

3. Position and pin the rickrack in place along the banner as shown. Sew through the center of the rickrack using a straight stitch and a walking foot.

4. Arrange the small stars on top of the rickrack and fuse in place, being careful not to scorch the rickrack. Arrange the large stars at the top of the banner and fuse in place. Using a blanket stitch and matching thread, appliqué the edges by hand or machine.

1½"

5. Referring to "Hand Embroidery" on page 9, hand stitch mouths on the snowmen.

APPLIQUÉING THE BANNER

1. Referring to "Fusible Appliqué" on page 8, use the patterns on pages 65 and 66 to prepare the following:
   - 4 snowmen from white flannel
   - 8 arms (4 of each) from brown print
   - 6 small stars and 3 large stars from gold flannel
   - 4 noses from orange flannel
   - 4 scarves from red flannel
   - 1 hat from brown-check flannel
   - 1 hatband from red flannel

2. Arrange all the shapes except for the stars onto the dark-brown 12" x 50" strip referring to the diagram at right and photo above

FINISHING THE BANNER

1. Layer the dark-brown 20" x 58" backing strip, the batting, and the banner top. Baste.

2. Quilt as desired. Our banner is machine quilted around each shape to define the individual pieces and make the snowmen pop.

3. Bind the banner using the dark-brown 2½"-wide strips. Refer to "Binding" on page 11 as needed.

4. Sew the black buttons on for eyes and gold buttons along the length of the rickrack, plus one on the hatband. Sew one red button to each snowman.

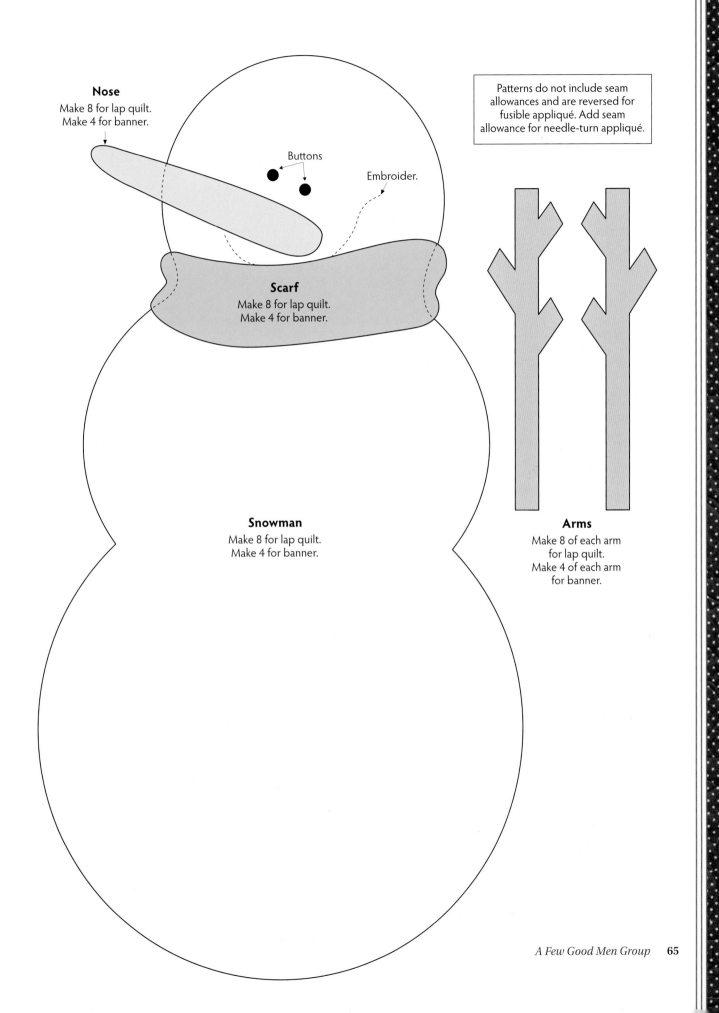

Nose
Make 8 for lap quilt.
Make 4 for banner.

Buttons

Embroider.

Patterns do not include seam
allowances and are reversed for
fusible appliqué. Add seam
allowance for needle-turn appliqué.

Scarf
Make 8 for lap quilt.
Make 4 for banner.

Snowman
Make 8 for lap quilt.
Make 4 for banner.

Arms
Make 8 of each arm
for lap quilt.
Make 4 of each arm
for banner.

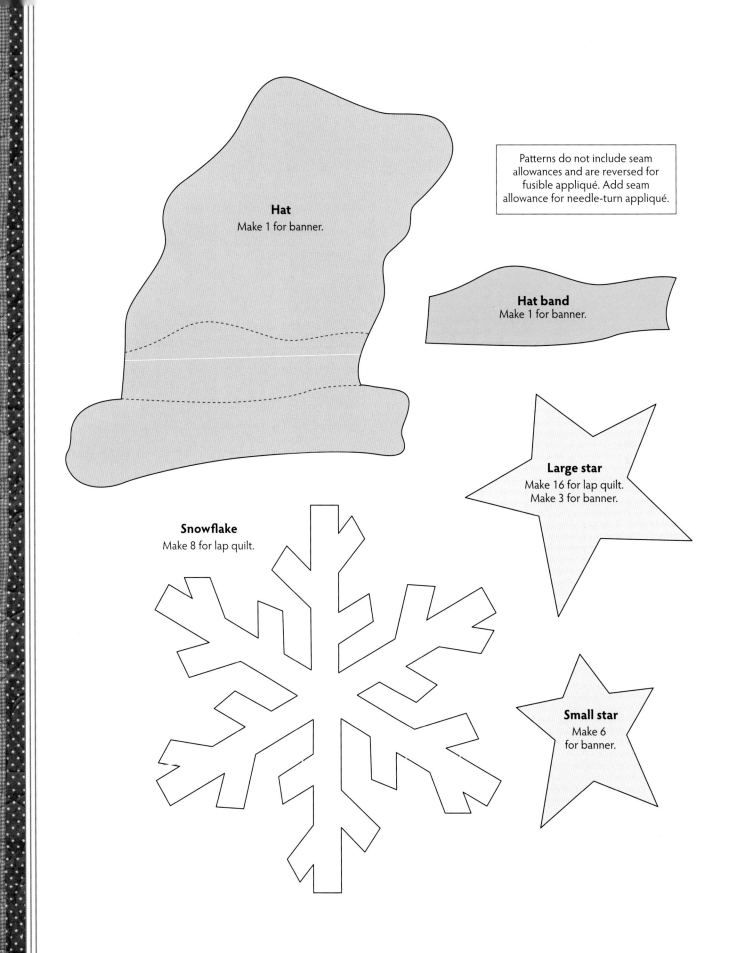

Hat
Make 1 for banner.

Patterns do not include seam allowances and are reversed for fusible appliqué. Add seam allowance for needle-turn appliqué.

Hat band
Make 1 for banner.

Large star
Make 16 for lap quilt.
Make 3 for banner.

Snowflake
Make 8 for lap quilt.

Small star
Make 6
for banner.

Joy-Peace-Believe Pillow Trio

This trio of pillows will complement your holiday decorating. Make one or make all three to accessorize your room for instant cheer. They also make great gifts!

FINISHED PILLOW: 14" x 22"

MATERIALS FOR ONE PILLOW

Yardage is based on 42"-wide fabric. Fat quarters measure approximately 18" x 21".

⅔ yard of gray flannel for outer border and pillow back

12" x 21" piece of black flannel for appliqué background

7" x 18" piece of red flannel for words

7" x 7" piece of gold flannel for stars

½ yard of 18"-wide lightweight fusible web

Matching thread for appliqué

2-pound bag of polyester stuffing

CUTTING

Cut all strips across the width of the fabric.

From the black flannel, cut:
1 rectangle, 10½" x 18½"

From the gray flannel, cut:
2 strips, 2½" x 42"; crosscut *each* strip into:
    1 strip, 2½" x 10½" (2 total)
    1 strip, 2½" x 22½" (2 total)
1 rectangle, 14½" x 22½"

"Joy-Peace-Believe Pillow Trio," designed and made by Shelley Wicks and Jeanne Large.

APPLIQUÉING THE PILLOW TOP

1. Referring to "Fusible Appliqué" on page 8, use the patterns on pages 70 and 71 to prepare four stars and the word *Believe, Joy,* or *Peace* for the pillow.

2. Arrange the letters and stars onto the black 10½" x 18½" rectangle as shown and fuse in place. Using a blanket stitch and black thread, appliqué the edges by hand or machine.

Appliqué placement

FINISHING THE PILLOW

1. Sew a gray 10½"-long strip to each side of the appliqué panel. Sew the gray 22½"-long strips to the top and bottom of the appliqué panel. Press the seam allowances toward the gray strips.

2. Lay the pillow top flat and place the gray 14½" x 22½" pillow back on top with right sides together. Sew all around the edges using a ¼" seam allowance and leaving a 4" opening along the bottom edge. Turn the pillow right side out, stuff firmly, and sew the opening closed by hand.

4"

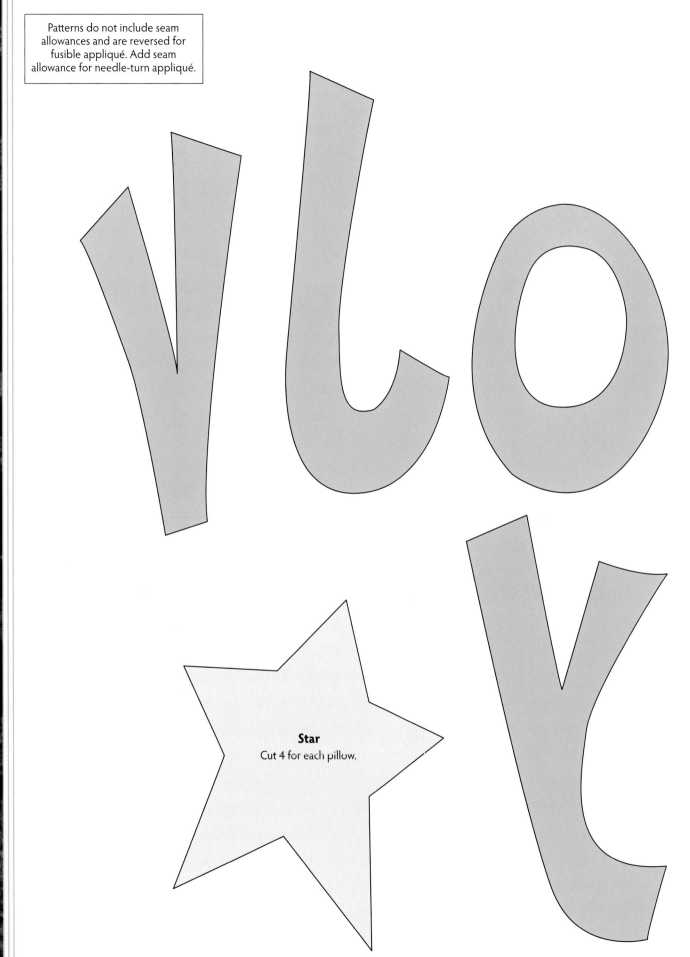

Star
Cut 4 for each pillow.

Merry, Merry Duo

*L*et your holiday spirit loose with the rich and warm colors of the season. This large quilt would be perfect to feature over the back of a couch, on a wall, or even as a table cover. Make the coordinating table runner to complete your warm holiday look.

Merry, Merry Lap Quilt

FINISHED QUILT: 66½" x 66½"

MATERIALS

Yardage is based on 42"-wide fabric. Fat quarters measure approximately 18" x 21".

1⅝ yards of gold tone on tone for appliquéd border and binding

1 yard of black print for borders

1 yard of red print for outer border

4 fat quarters of assorted red prints for checkerboard and Nine Patch blocks

4 fat quarters of assorted gold prints for checkerboard and Nine Patch blocks

1 fat quarter of light-gold print for stars

8" x 24" piece *each* of 3 green prints for holly leaves

6" x 9" piece of red print for berries

4¼ yards of fabric for backing

75" x 75" piece of batting

5 yards of ½"-wide green rickrack

1½ yards of 18"-wide lightweight fusible web

Matching thread for appliqué

CUTTING

Cut all strips across the width of the fabric.

From *each* of the red fat quarters, cut:
3 strips, 4½" x 21"; crosscut the strips into
    11 squares, 4½" x 4½" (44 total, 2 are extra)
1 strip, 2½" x 21"; crosscut the strip into 5
    squares, 2½" x 2½" (20 total)

From *each* of the gold fat quarters, cut:
3 strips, 4½" x 21"; crosscut the strips into
    11 squares, 4½" x 4½" (44 total, 2 are extra)
1 strip, 2½" x 21"; crosscut the strip into 4
    squares, 2½" x 2½" (16 total)

From the black print, cut:
10 strips, 2½" x 42"; crosscut *4 of the strips* into:
    2 strips, 2½" x 34½"
    2 strips, 2½" x 38½"
4 strips, 1½" x 42"; crosscut the strips into:
    8 strips, 1½" x 6½"
    8 strips, 1½" x 8½"

From the gold tone on tone, cut:
4 strips, 8½" x 42"; crosscut the strips into
    4 strips, 8½" x 38½"
7 strips, 2½" x 42"

From the red print, cut:
7 strips, 4½" x 42"

"Merry, Merry Lap Quilt," designed and made by Shelley Wicks and Jeanne Large, machine quilted by Wendy Findlay.

PIECING THE QUILT CENTER

1. Lay out the 42 red and 42 gold 4½" squares on point as shown. Sew the squares together in diagonal rows, starting in one corner and working across to the opposite corner. Press the seam allowances in opposite directions from row to row. Sew the rows together. Press the seam allowances in one direction.

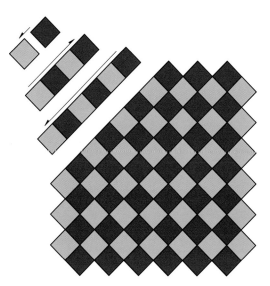

2. Trim the edges of the quilt center so that it measures 34½" x 34½". Be sure to leave ¼" beyond the corners of the squares.

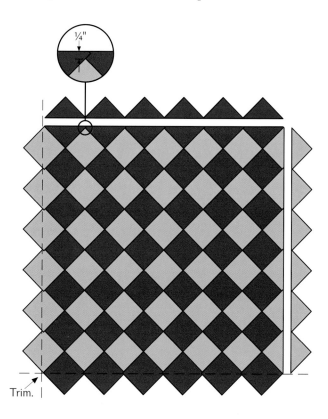

PIECING THE NINE PATCH BLOCKS

1. Lay out five red and four gold 2½" squares to make a Nine Patch block as shown. Sew the squares together into rows. Press the seam allowances toward the red squares. Sew the rows together to make the block. Press the seam allowances in one direction. Make four Nine Patch blocks.

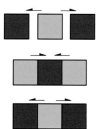

Make 4.

2. Sew a black 1½" x 6½" strip to each side of a Nine Patch block. Sew black 1½" x 8½" strips to the top and bottom of the block. Press the seam allowances toward the black strips. Repeat with all four blocks.

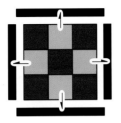

APPLIQUÉING THE BORDERS

1. Place a length of rickrack on a gold 8½" x 38½" border strip, forming a gentle curve. Referring to "Using Rickrack" on page 9, pin the rickrack in place and trim the excess length. Sew the rickrack down. Repeat for each of the gold border strips.

2. Referring to "Fusible Appliqué" on page 8, use the patterns on page 79 to prepare the following:
   - 8 holly leaves from *each* green print (24 total)
   - 24 berries from red print
   - 16 stars from light-gold print

3. Arrange the shapes onto the gold border strips as shown. Fuse in place. Use matching thread to blanket stitch around each shape by hand or machine.

Make 4.

ADDING THE BORDERS

1. Sew the black 2½" x 34½" strips to opposite sides of the quilt center. Sew the black 2½" x 38½" strips to the top and bottom of the quilt center. Press the seam allowances toward the black border.

2. Sew a gold appliquéd border strip to each side of the quilt center. Sew a Nine Patch block to each end of the remaining two appliquéd border strips. Press the seam allowances toward the appliquéd border strips. Sew the borders to the top and bottom of the quilt. Press the seam allowances toward the appliquéd border.

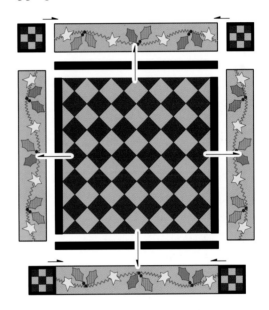

3. Sew the six black 2½" x 42" strips end to end to make one long continuous strip. From this strip, cut two strips, 54½" long, and two strips, 58½" long. Sew a black 54½"-long strip to each side of the quilt. Sew the black 58½"-long strips to the top and bottom of the quilt. Press the seam allowances toward the black border.

4. Sew the seven red 4½" x 42" strips end to end to make one long continuous strip and cut two strips, 58½" long, and two strips, 66½" long. Sew a red 58½"-long border strip to each side of the quilt. Sew the 66½"-long strips to the top and bottom of the quilt. Press the seam allowances toward the red border.

Quilt assembly

FINISHING THE QUILT

1. Layer the backing, batting, and quilt top; baste.

2. Quilt as desired. Our quilt is machine quilted with an allover design.

3. Bind the quilt using the gold 2½"-wide strips. Refer to "Binding" on page 11 as needed.

Merry, Merry Table Runner

FINISHED RUNNER: 38½" x 18½"

MATERIALS

Yardage is based on 42"-wide fabric. Fat eighths measure approximately 9" x 21".

½ yard of black print for inner border and binding

⅓ yard of red print for outer border

¼ yard *each* of 4 assorted gold prints for background*

1 fat eighth of black print for letters

9" x 12" piece of light-gold print for stars

8" x 12" piece of green print for holly leaves

4" x 4" piece of red print for berries

1⅓ yards of fabric for backing

26" x 46" piece of batting

1⅛ yards of ½"-wide green rickrack

¾ yard of 18"-wide lightweight fusible web

Matching thread for appliqué

Number the gold prints from 1 to 4. Gold print #4 will be the background for the appliquéd words.

CUTTING

Cut all strips across the width of the fabric.

From gold print #1, cut:

1 strip, 4½" x 42"; crosscut the strip into:
- 2 squares, 4½" x 4½"
- 2 rectangles, 4½" x 8½"

From gold print #2, cut:

1 strip, 4½" x 42"; crosscut the strip into:
- 1 square, 4½" x 4½"
- 2 rectangles, 4½" x 8½"

From gold print #3, cut:

1 strip, 4½" x 42"; crosscut the strip into:
- 1 square, 4½" x 4½"
- 2 rectangles, 4½" x 8½"

From gold print #4, cut:

1 strip, 4½" x 42"; crosscut the strip into
- 2 rectangles, 4½" x 16½"

From the black print, cut:

3 strips, 1½" x 42"; crosscut the strips into:
- 2 strips, 1½" x 14½"
- 2 strips, 1½" x 32½"

3 strips, 2½" x 42"

From the red print, cut:

3 strips, 2½" x 42"; crosscut the strips into:
- 2 strips, 2½" x 18½"
- 2 strips, 2½" x 34½"

"Merry, Merry Table Runner," designed and made by Shelley Wicks and Jeanne Large, machine quilted by Jeanne Large.

ASSEMBLING THE TABLE RUNNER

1. Lay out the gold squares and rectangles as shown. Sew them together into rows. Press the seam allowances in opposite directions from row to row. Sew the rows together. Press the seam allowances in one direction.

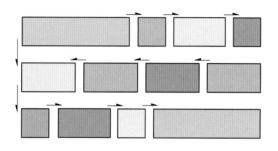

2. Refer to "Using Rickrack" on page 9 for more detailed instructions. Lay the rickrack on the pieced background, shaping it into a gentle curve. Pin in place, trim the excess, and sew down the center of the rickrack using a straight stitch and a walking foot.

3. Referring to "Fusible Appliqué" on page 8, use the patterns on page 79 to prepare the following:
   - 4 sets of letters for *Merry* from black print
   - 4 holly leaves from green print
   - 4 stars from light-gold print
   - 4 berries from red print

4. Using the photo on page 77 as a guide, position and fuse the shapes in place on the pieced background. Be sure that you leave at least 1" between the words and the raw edge of the pieced background. Use matching thread to blanket stitch around each shape by hand or machine.

5. Sew the black 1½" x 32½" inner-border strips to the long sides of the runner. Sew the black 1½" x 14½" strips to the short sides of the runner. Press the seam allowances toward the black border.

6. Sew the red 2½" x 34½" outer-border strips to the long sides of the runner. Sew the red 2½" x 18½" strips to the short sides of the runner. Press the seam allowances toward the red border.

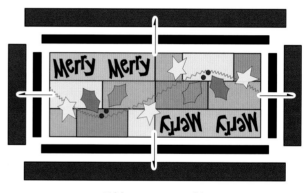

Table-runner assembly

FINISHING THE TABLE RUNNER

1. Layer the backing, batting, and table-runner top; baste.

2. Quilt as desired. Our table runner is machine quilted in the ditch and around the shapes.

3. Bind the table runner using the black 2½"-wide strips. Refer to "Binding" on page 11 as needed.

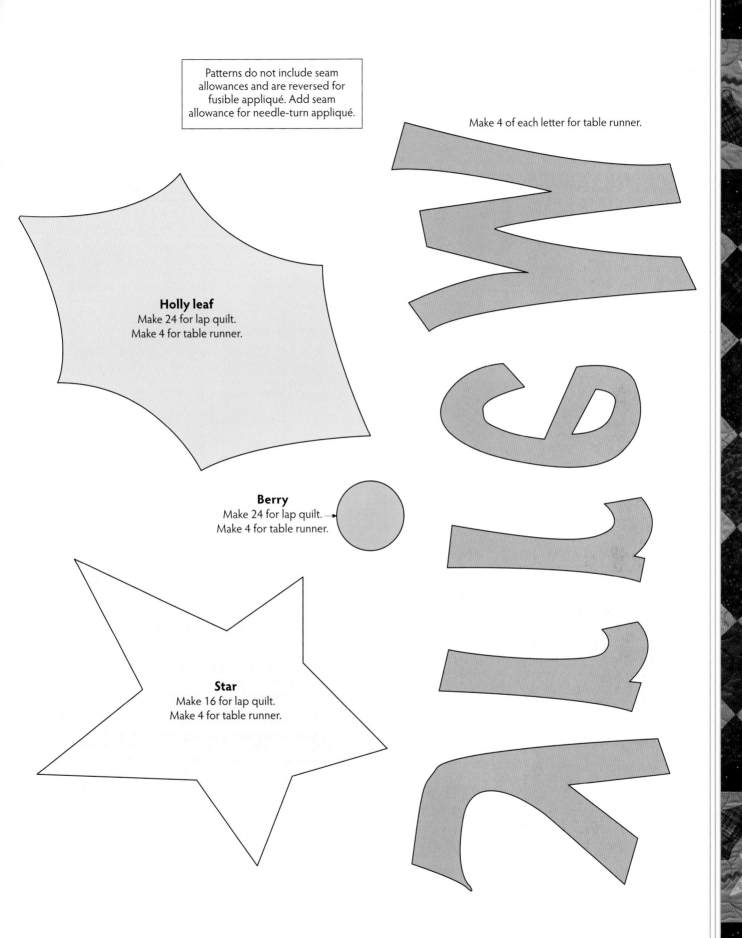

Patterns do not include seam allowances and are reversed for fusible appliqué. Add seam allowance for needle-turn appliqué.

Make 4 of each letter for table runner.

Holly leaf
Make 24 for lap quilt.
Make 4 for table runner.

Berry
Make 24 for lap quilt.
Make 4 for table runner.

Star
Make 16 for lap quilt.
Make 4 for table runner.

Snow Happy Family

Who doesn't love a snowman? This winter, make your home "snow happy" with this cute little duo! Table toppers are quick to make and add instant cheer. The juggling snowman on the door banner will welcome all who enter.

Snow Happy Table Topper

FINISHED QUILT: 21" x 21"

MATERIALS

Yardage is based on 42"-wide fabric. Fat eighths measure approximately 9" x 21".

¾ yard of charcoal-gray flannel for blocks, sashing, and binding

1 fat eighth of white flannel for snowmen

6" x 10" piece *each* of 2 green flannels for scarves and circles

6" x 10" piece *each* of 2 red flannels for scarves and circles

7" x 7" piece of brown flannel for arms

4" x 5" piece of gold flannel for star

2" x 5" piece of orange flannel for noses

1 yard of fabric for backing

29" x 29" piece of batting

⅞ yard of 18"-wide lightweight fusible web

Matching thread for appliqué

CUTTING

Cut all strips across the width of the fabric.

From the charcoal-gray flannel, cut:

1 strip, 9½" x 42"; crosscut the strip into 4 squares, 9½" x 9½"

1 strip, 3" x 42"; crosscut the strip into 4 rectangles, 3" x 9½"

1 square, 3" x 3"

3 strips, 2½" x 42"

"Snow Happy Table Topper," designed and made by Shelley Wicks and Jeanne Large, machine quilted by Jeanne Large.

APPLIQUÉING THE QUILT

1. Referring to "Fusible Appliqué" on page 8, use the patterns on page 85 to prepare the following:
   - ◆ 4 snowmen from white flannel
   - ◆ 1 scarf, 2 large circles, and 2 small circles from *each* red flannel
   - ◆ 1 scarf, 2 large circles, and 2 small circles from *each* green flannel
   - ◆ 4 noses from orange flannel
   - ◆ 8 arms (4 of each) from brown flannel
   - ◆ 1 star from gold flannel

2. Arrange the circles on the charcoal-gray 3" x 9½" rectangles as shown and fuse in place. Position a snowman, scarf, nose, and two arms on each of the charcoal-gray 9½" squares as shown and fuse in place. Using a blanket stitch and matching thread, appliqué the edges by hand or machine. Refer to "Machine Embroidery" on page 9 for detailed instructions on embroidering the snowman's eyes and mouth. The star will be appliquéd after the table topper is put together.

Make 4.

Make 4.

ASSEMBLING THE QUILT

1. Arrange the blocks, sashing, and 3" square in rows as shown. Sew the blocks together into rows, pressing the seam allowances toward the appliquéd sashing. Sew the rows together to form the table topper. Press the seam allowances toward the sashing.

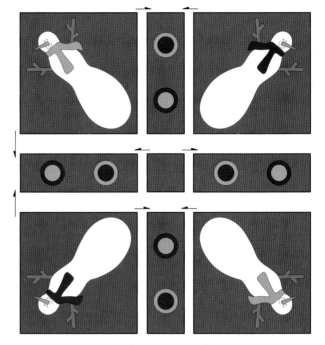

Table-topper assembly

2. Place the gold star in the center and fuse in place. Using a blanket stitch and matching thread, appliqué the edges by hand or machine.

FINISHING THE QUILT

1. Layer the backing, batting, and quilt top; baste.

2. Quilt as desired. Our quilt is machine quilted in the ditch.

3. Bind the quilt using the charcoal-gray 2½"-wide strips. Refer to "Binding" on page 11 as needed.

Snow Happy Door Banner

FINISHED BANNER: 6" x 18"

MATERIALS

Yardage is based on 42"-wide fabric.

¼ yard of charcoal-gray flannel for front
    and back

5" x 10" piece of white flannel for snowman

4" x 5" piece of gold flannel for star

4" x 4" piece of red flannel for scarf

4" x 4" piece of brown flannel for arms

2" x 2" piece of orange flannel for nose

4 white buttons, ½" diameter

14" piece of ½"-wide black rickrack (½ yard)

¼ yard of 20"-wide fusible fleece

⅓ yard of 18"-wide, lightweight fusible web

1 silver bell, 1¼" diameter

Matching thread for appliqué

Charcoal-gray thread for topstitching

CUTTING

Cut all strips across the width of the fabric.

From the charcoal-gray flannel, cut:
1 strip, 6½" x 42"; crosscut the strip into
    2 rectangles, 6½" x 18½"

From the fusible fleece, cut:
2 rectangles, 6½" x 18½"

"Snow Happy Door Banner," designed and made by Shelley Wicks and Jeanne Large.

83

ASSEMBLING THE BANNER

1. Place a fusible-fleece rectangle on the wrong side of each charcoal-gray flannel rectangle and fuse, following the manufacturer's instructions.

2. Find the center point along the bottom edge of the rectangle. Draw a line at a 60° angle from this point to each side edge, measuring up each side 5⅝". The line will be 6½" long. Cut along both lines to create the shape at the bottom of the hanger. Repeat with the second rectangle.

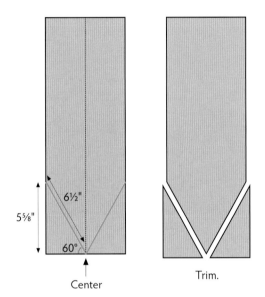

3. Referring to "Fusible Appliqué" on page 8, use the patterns on page 85 to prepare the following:
   - 1 snowman from white flannel
   - 1 scarf from red flannel
   - 1 nose from orange flannel
   - 1 star from gold flannel
   - 2 arms (1 of each) from brown flannel

4. Using the photo on page 83 as a guide, arrange the shapes onto one of the charcoal-gray background pieces and fuse in place. Using a blanket stitch and matching thread, appliqué the edges by hand or machine. Refer to "Machine Embroidery" on page 9 for detailed instructions on embroidering the snowman's eyes and mouth. Hand stitch the buttons on.

5. Lay the appliquéd flannel piece right side up. Place the rickrack in a U shape along the top, aligning the ends with the top edge of the flannel piece. Layer the remaining piece of gray flannel on top, with right sides together. Pin in place. Sew all around the edges using a ¼" seam allowance and leaving a 4" opening along one side for turning. Trim diagonally across the corners and turn the banner right side out. Press the banner carefully so the edges are nice and flat.

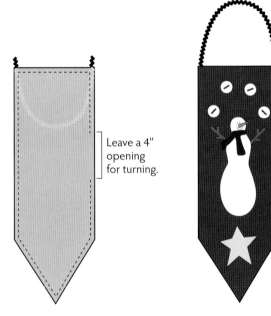

6. Using a ⅛" seam allowance and charcoal-gray thread, topstitch all around the edges.

7. Stitch the bell onto the bottom of the banner by hand.

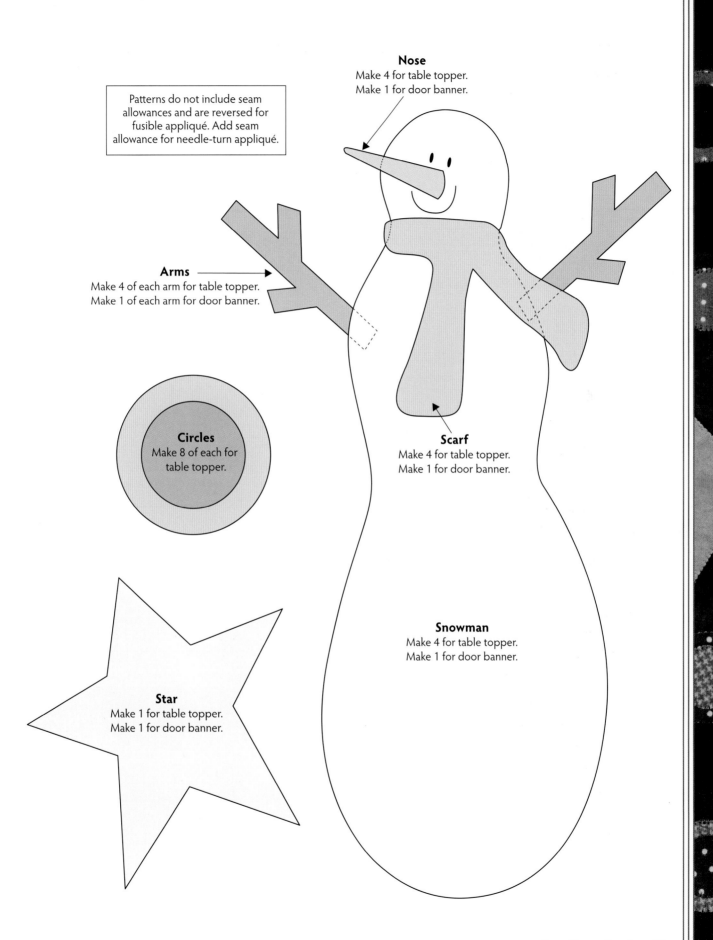

Patterns do not include seam allowances and are reversed for fusible appliqué. Add seam allowance for needle-turn appliqué.

Nose
Make 4 for table topper.
Make 1 for door banner.

Arms
Make 4 of each arm for table topper.
Make 1 of each arm for door banner.

Circles
Make 8 of each for table topper.

Scarf
Make 4 for table topper.
Make 1 for door banner.

Snowman
Make 4 for table topper.
Make 1 for door banner.

Star
Make 1 for table topper.
Make 1 for door banner.

"It's Cold Outside Lap Quilt," designed and made by Shelley Wicks
and Jeanne Large, machine quilted by Wendy Findlay.

It's Cold Outside

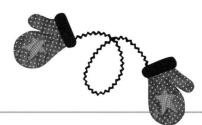

In our part of the world, it's cold outside for several months of the year, so a pair of fuzzy, warm mittens is an important item in everyone's winter wardrobe! Rickrack strings are just the ticket to keep those pairs together.

FINISHED QUILT: 56½" x 56½" ◆ FINISHED BLOCK: 20" x 20"

MATERIALS

Yardage is based on 42"-wide fabric. Fat eighths measure approximately 9" x 21".

1⅝ yards of light-gray flannel for appliqué background and outer border

1 yard of black flannel for inner border and binding

½ yard of gray flannel for sashing

4 fat eighths of assorted green flannels for blocks

3 fat eighths of assorted red flannels for blocks

3 fat eighths of assorted blue flannels for blocks

6" x 18" piece of gold flannel for stars

7" x 11" piece *each* of 2 red flannels for mittens and cuffs

7" x 11" piece of green flannel for mittens and cuffs

7" x 11" piece of blue flannel for mittens and cuffs

8" x 8" piece of black flannel for circle

3⅔ yards of fabric for backing

65" x 65" piece of batting

2¾ yards of ⅜"-wide black rickrack

2½ yards of 1½"-wide red rickrack

1 yard of 18"-wide lightweight fusible web

Matching thread for appliqué

CUTTING

Cut all strips across the width of the fabric.

From *each* of the red, green, and blue fat eighths, cut:

2 strips, 3½" x 21" (20 total); crosscut the strips into 8 rectangles, 3½" x 4½" (80 total)

From the light-gray flannel, cut:

2 strips, 8½" x 42"; crosscut the strips into 4 strips, 8½" x 20½"

6 strips, 4½" x 42"

From the gray flannel, cut:

3 strips, 4½" x 42"; crosscut the strips into 4 strips, 4½" x 20½"

1 square, 4½" x 4½"

From the black flannel, cut:

11 strips, 2½" x 42"

ASSEMBLING THE QUILT TOP

1. Arrange 20 red, green, and blue 3½" x 4½" rectangles in five rows of four rectangles each. Sew the rectangles together into rows. Press the seam allowances in opposite directions from row to row. Sew the rows together to make a section. Press the seam allowances in one direction. Make four sections.

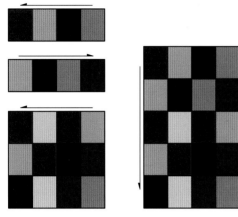

Make 4.

2. Cut the black rickrack into four pieces, 24" long. Referring to "Using Rickrack" on page 9, position one length of rickrack on a light-gray 8½" x 20½" rectangle as shown, forming a gentle loop. Pin in place and then sew the rickrack down. Make four.

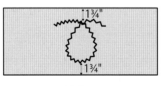

Make 4.

3. Position the red rickrack in a straight line through the center of a gray 4½" x 20½" strip. Sew the rickrack along both edges. Make four sashing strips.

Make 4.

4. Referring to "Fusible Appliqué" on page 8, use the patterns on page 90 to prepare the following from the 7" x 11" pieces of flannel:
   - 1 mitten and 1 reversed from *each* red flannel
   - 2 cuffs from *each* red flannel
   - 1 mitten and 1 reversed from green flannel
   - 2 cuffs from green flannel
   - 1 mitten and 1 reversed from blue flannel
   - 2 cuffs from blue flannel
   - 8 small stars and 1 large star from gold flannel
   - 1 circle from black flannel

5. Arrange the mittens, cuffs, and stars onto each light-gray rectangle as shown. Fuse in place. Use matching thread to blanket stitch around each shape by hand or machine.

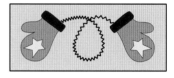

Appliqué placement

6. Sew a mitten rectangle to a pieced section as shown. Press the seam allowances toward the mittens. Make four sections.

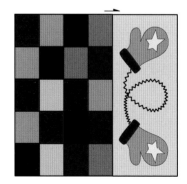

Make 4.

7. Lay out the four sections from step 6 with four sashing strips and the gray 4½" square, rotating each section a quarter turn as shown. Sew the sections and sashing strips together in rows. Press the seam allowances toward the sashing. Sew the sashing strips to each end of the gray center square. Press the seam allowances toward the sashing. Sew the rows together and press the seam allowances toward the sashing.

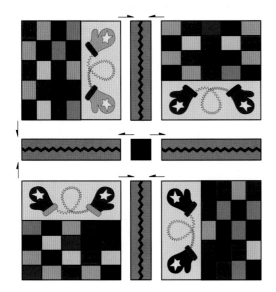

ADDING THE BORDERS

1. Sew five of the black 2½" x 42" strips end to end to make one long continuous strip. From this strip, cut two strips, 2½" x 44½", and two strips, 2½" x 48½". Sew the 44½"-long strips to opposite sides of the quilt top. Sew the 48½"-long strips to the top and bottom of the quilt top. Press the seam allowances toward the black border.

2. Sew the light-gray 4½" x 42" strips end to end to make one long continuous strip. From this strip, cut two strips, 4½" x 48½", and two strips, 4½" x 56½". Sew a 48½"-long strip to each side of the quilt. Sew the 56½"-long strips to the top and bottom of the quilt. Press the seam allowances toward the gray border.

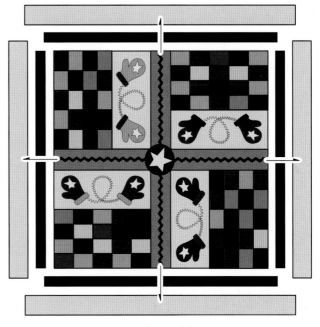

Quilt assembly

FINISHING THE QUILT

1. Layer the backing, batting, and quilt top; baste.

2. Quilt as desired. Our quilt is machine quilted with an allover design.

3. Bind the quilt using the remaining black 2½"-wide strips. Refer to "Binding" on page 11 as needed.

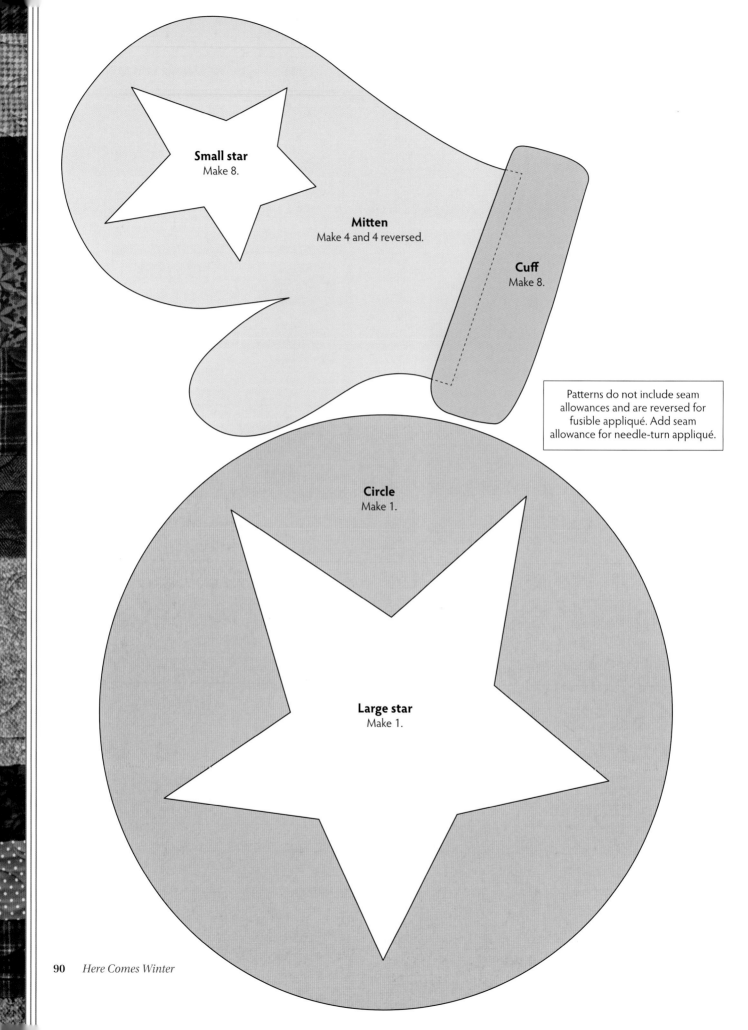

Small star
Make 8.

Mitten
Make 4 and 4 reversed.

Cuff
Make 8.

Patterns do not include seam allowances and are reversed for fusible appliqué. Add seam allowance for needle-turn appliqué.

Circle
Make 1.

Large star
Make 1.

Lost Mittens

ittens, mittens everywhere, but never a matching pair. Who isn't familiar with this scenario? Whether they match or not, it's our opinion that you can never have enough mittens!

FINISHED WALL HANGING: 20½" x 18½"

MATERIALS

Yardage is based on 42"-wide fabric. Fat eighths measure approximately 9" x 21".

½ yard of gray print for top and bottom borders and binding

1 fat eighth of green print for checkerboard

1 fat eighth of red print for checkerboard

⅛ yard of black solid for border

4" x 20" piece of black solid for letters

3" x 10" piece of gold print for stars

4" x 5" piece *each* of 2 red prints for mittens

4" x 5" piece *each* of 2 green prints for mittens

¾ yard of fabric for backing

26" x 28" piece of batting

20" of 1½"-wide red rickrack (⅝ yard)

⅝ yard of 18"-wide lightweight fusible web

Matching thread for appliqué

2 red and 2 green buttons, ¾" diameter

CUTTING

Cut all strips across the width of the fabric.

From *each* of the red and green fat eighths, cut:
2 strips, 3½" x 21" (4 total)

From the gray print, cut:
1 strip, 4½" x 42"; crosscut the strip into 2 strips, 4½" x 18½"
3 strips, 2½" x 42"

From the black solid, cut:
2 strips, 1½" x 42"; crosscut the strips into 4 strips, 1½" x 18½"

"Lost Mittens," designed and made by Shelley Wicks and Jeanne Large, machine quilted by Jeanne Large.

ASSEMBLING THE WALL HANGING

1. Sew one red and one green 3½" x 21" strip together along the long edge to make a strip set. Press the seam allowances toward the green strip. Repeat with the remaining red and green strips to make two strip sets. Crosscut the strip sets into six segments, 4½" wide.

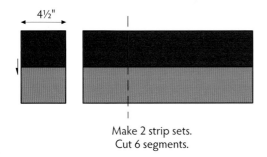

4½"

Make 2 strip sets.
Cut 6 segments.

2. Sew the segments together in rows as shown; press the seam allowances toward the green print. Sew the rows together and press the seam allowances in one direction. The unit should measure 8½" x 18½".

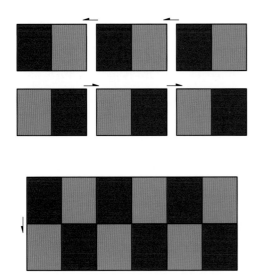

3. Place a length of rickrack along the raw edge of the unit from step 2 so that the rickrack's inner curve is aligned with the outer edge of the wall hanging and the outer curve is off the wall hanging. Pin in place and sew using a small zigzag stitch, keeping one edge of the stitch along the outer edge of the wall hanging. Using a rotary cutter and ruler, trim along the outer edge of the checkerboard section, cutting off the excess rickrack (the outer curves).

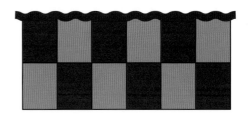

4. Place a gray 4½" x 18½" strip right sides together on top of the pieced center section, aligning the raw edges. Pin in place. Sew along the edge. Press the seam allowances toward the gray strip. Sew the remaining gray 4½" x 18½" strip to the bottom of the pieced center section. Press the seam allowances toward the gray strip.

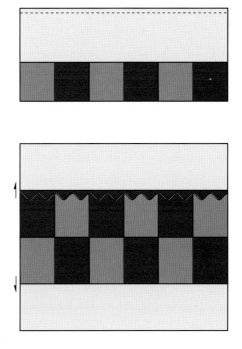

5. Referring to "Fusible Appliqué" on page 8, use the patterns on page 95 to prepare the following from the 4" x 5" pieces of red and green prints:

   - 3 stars from gold print
   - 1 mitten from red print
   - 1 mitten reversed from a second red print
   - 1 mitten from *each* green print
   - Letters for *lost mittens* from black solid

6. Using the photo on page 92 as a guide, arrange the shapes onto the pieced unit from step 4. Fuse in place. Use black thread to blanket stitch around each shape by hand or machine.

7. Sew the black 1½" x 18½" strips to the top and bottom of the wall hanging. Sew the remaining two black 1½" x 18½" strips to the sides of the wall hanging. Press the seam allowances toward the black border.

FINISHING THE WALL HANGING

1. Layer the backing, batting, and wall-hanging top; baste.

2. Quilt as desired. Our wall hanging is machine quilted in the ditch.

3. Bind the wall hanging using the gray 2½"-wide strips. Refer to "Binding" on page 11 as needed.

4. Sew the buttons on by hand.

Pillow Option

This project would also make a very cute pillow. Before attaching the binding, make a pillow backing using two pieces of fabric, 18½" x 14½". Turn under ½" on one long side of each backing rectangle. Stitch ¼" from the fold. Lay the backing pieces under the pillow top, wrong sides together and outer edges even with the pillow top. The hemmed edges will overlap in the center. Sew all around the outer edges of the pillow using a ¼" seam allowance. Attach the binding. Insert an 18" x 20" pillow form, and voilà!

Make 1 of each letter.

Patterns do not include seam allowances and are reversed for fusible appliqué. Add seam allowance for needle-turn appliqué.

Star
Make 3.

Mitten
Make 3 and 1 reversed.

About the Authors

Shelley Wicks and Jeanne Large have owned The Quilt Patch in Moose Jaw, Saskatchewan, Canada, since 2002. Along with the day-to-day running of the quilt shop, these women also design and make almost every quilt that hangs in their shop.

Twice a year, spring and fall, Shelley and Jeanne unveil a brand-new collection of projects with that modern country look that appeals to customers of all ages. Their customers enjoy the continuing change of quilts in the shop and know that there will always be something new to see.

With their first three books, *'Tis the Season, Urban Country Quilts,* and *'Tis the Autumn Season* (Martingale, 2010, 2011, and

Shelley and Jeanne

2013, respectively), Shelley and Jeanne introduced the chunky appliqué, easy piecing, and earth-toned projects that are the basis of their style to a wider audience. Their designs give customers the confidence that each project will be something that they can accomplish easily and will look fabulous in their home.

Every step of their adventure is met head-on with passion and energy that fuels the daily workload and fills it with laughter and fun. Both these women love what they do, and it shows in everything they accomplish.

Find out more about Shelley and Jeanne by visiting their website: www.TheQuiltPatch.ca.